UNIVERSITY OF CHICAGO STUDIES IN LIBRARY SCIENCE

THE INTELLECTUAL FOUNDATIONS OF LIBRARY EDUCATION

THE INTELLECTUAL FOUNDATIONS OF LIBRARY EDUCATION

*The Twenty-ninth Annual Conference
of the Graduate Library School
July 6–8, 1964*

Edited by DON R. SWANSON

THE UNIVERSITY OF CHICAGO PRESS
CHICAGO AND LONDON

The papers in this volume were published originally in the LIBRARY QUARTERLY, *October 1964. Thanks are tendered to the Joseph Fels Foundation, Inc., for financial support of the Conference from which these Proceedings came.*

The University of Chicago Press, Chicago & London
The University of Toronto Press, Toronto 5, Canada

Copyright 1965 by The University of Chicago
All rights reserved. Published 1965
Composed and printed by THE UNIVERSITY OF CHICAGO PRESS
Chicago, Illinois, U.S.A.

TABLE OF CONTENTS

INTRODUCTION 1
    Don R. Swanson, *Dean, Graduate Library School, University of Chicago*

THE AGE OF THE SYMBOL—A PHILOSOPHY OF LIBRARY EDUCATION . . 7
    Abraham Kaplan, *Professor, Department of Philosophy, University of Michigan*

THE STUDY OF THE USE AND USERS OF RECORDED KNOWLEDGE . . 17
    Philip H. Ennis, *Assistant Professor, Graduate Library School, University of Chicago*

THE ROLE OF THE PUBLIC LIBRARY: IMPLICATIONS FOR LIBRARY EDUCATION 27
    Leon Carnovsky, *Professor, Graduate Library School, University of Chicago*

THE SYSTEMS APPROACH TO LIBRARY PLANNING 38
    Merrill M. Flood, *Professor, Mental Health Research Institute, University of Michigan*

THE DEVELOPMENT OF A METHODOLOGY FOR SYSTEM DESIGN AND ITS ROLE IN LIBRARY EDUCATION 51
    Robert M. Hayes, *Professor in Residence, School of Library Service, University of California at Los Angeles*

THEORETICAL PRINCIPLES OF INFORMATION ORGANIZATION IN LIBRARIANSHIP 64
    Vladimir Slamecka, *Director, School of Information Science, Georgia Institute of Technology*
    Mortimer Taube, *Chairman of the Board, Documentation Incorporated*

LIBRARY EDUCATION: THE ROLE OF CLASSIFICATION, INDEXING, AND SUBJECT ANALYSIS 74
    D. J. Foskett, *Librarian, University of London Institute of Education, London*

    COMMENT 85
        Harold Borko, *Information Retrieval and Linguistics Staff, System Development Corporation, Santa Monica, California*

THE LIBRARIAN'S ROLE IN THE DEVELOPMENT OF LIBRARY BOOK COLLECTIONS 86
    Gordon Williams, *Director, Midwest Inter-Library Center, Chicago*

INTRODUCTION

DON R. SWANSON

IT IS almost self-evident that strong forces are operating to change the character of the library profession. Library education must concern itself profoundly with these changes, and so in the search for intellectual foundations our best point of beginning may well be to recognize and formulate future goals. Thus this conference will be as much concerned with libraries and librarians of the future as with education itself. This view, as persuasive as it seems to be, nevertheless presents a dilemma to the library school. Library education must be built upon sound intellectual foundations, but at the same time it cannot ignore the vocational skills needed in the practice of librarianship. These vocational needs of the profession are great, and the skills not difficult to recognize; but their intellectual content is often obscure and subject to divided opinion. We suggest here that this intellectual content is just that aspect that does stand the test of time. For education to respond solely to today's needs may result in failure to produce tomorrow's leaders, so the search for the proper foundations is of more than academic interest. Long-term goals for the profession must be formulated, and the student must be educated so that he has a freedom of choice in the pursuit of those goals. Pressures toward increasing specialization are a fact of life, but they cannot be accepted uncritically. Education must still open the maximum number of future doors for the student and teach him the skills that can be transferred from one specialty to another. The very proliferation of specialties assures that some will not endure.[1] Thus it is the task of this conference not to describe the vocational skills presently needed in librarianship, because for the most part these are well known, but to identify the principles common to various specialties that will have greatest significance in the shaping of future libraries and their services.

The fields of information science, information technology, information retrieval, and documentation will not be

---

[1] A viewpoint on special librarianship is presented by the author in "The Education of a Catalyst," *Special Libraries*, Vol. LV (October, 1964).

treated as separate topics but rather as an integral part of library science, especially insofar as they make their own contributions to our analysis of the intellectual foundations. Thus we shall not be concerned with whether information science is part of library science or vice versa, but rather we shall assume that the educational process in a graduate library school must adequately take both into account.

The conference has (with some malice aforethought) been divided into four major areas, with an implication that the intellectual foundations are to be sought therein. It should be understood though that no initially constructed framework can be adequate to represent the diversity of views likely to arise, nor is it intended that these four areas be looked upon as constraints. They do perhaps provide at least a pattern for the asking of questions, and an outline within which we might try to discern the shape of things to come.

SOCIETY AND THE USE OF LIBRARIES

Library goals and purposes can, of course, have significance only in the context of the needs and behavior of library users. In the past decade there has been much emphasis on research in this area, and a few important lessons have been learned. Librarians must have far more than the basic skills of cataloging and reference in order to take advantage of these lessons, however. An ability to appraise critically the results of research seems to be vital, and this ability alone presents no small challenge to the educational process.

Questions dealing with the role that libraries should play in the over-all process of communicating human knowledge provide a point of beginning for the development of "requirements" for the performance of libraries. A clear distinction between goals and their means of fulfilment is an essential prerequisite of sound planning for future systems. The very existence of libraries, for example, is not to be regarded as a goal, but rather as one means of fulfilling a requirement for information services. The following questions thus emphasize performance requirements, independently of any particular design or approach.

What kinds of new and improved services can be envisioned which could have significant impact on the future role of libraries in our society? To what extent does the demand for library services tend to rise as those services are improved?

What is the nature of the relationship between library quality and library use?

What has been the historical function of the library as an agency of culture?

Is selective initial dissemination of published material a direct responsibility of libraries; and if so, what would be the ultimate implications of such responsibility?

What characterizes readers; how many and what types of reading patterns are discernible in adults and children?

What communication channels for recorded information in our society are of particular significance to decision-making processes?

How are the use and the usefulness of a library affected by how rapidly it responds to requests?

Many studies on the use of information and libraries and on the behavior or needs of users have been carried out; what are the implications of this area of research for library education?

Is the role that libraries play in the communication of human knowledge likely to change significantly in the future; and if so, how should library education take account of such change?

SYSTEMS PLANNING AND ANALYSIS

Once library goals have been identified, it may be assumed there are many paths for reaching these goals. The study of different possible paths, the optimal allocation of resources (both human and machine), and the analysis of competing types of equipment, all are involved in the planning and analysis of systems. Thus we include here the study of automation, but with a recognition that automation is a means, not an end. The concept of alternative paths must be broad enough to include the possibility of radical changes in the concept of libraries as such, and broad enough to permit one to envision the information resources of the country as constituting a single system or a network. The systems analyst must be prepared, if necessary, to abandon or redefine traditional boundaries of libraries and of library services. His special ability must include the asking of the right questions.

What are the various possibilities for the organization and location of stored information and the means of transmitting such information to its point of use?

What measures can be developed for library effectiveness and how can these be incorporated in a system of quality control and feedback for improvement of services?

Can one economically provide for remote interrogation and/or remote delivery of library materials?

How does the cost of a library or other information service vary with response time and with the rate at which requests for information are placed?

Is "on-line" interrogation of bibliographic tools (if they are mechanized) necessary; or can requests be processed in batches? What are the economic implications in each case?

What are the relative advantages, disadvantages, and economics of book catalogs, card catalogs, and computerized catalogs?

If a library request is envisioned as a dialogue,[2] what requirements does this impose on the design of a system for providing this capability?

How do the issues of miniaturization differ from those of computer applications in libraries; what is the significance of each for basic improvements in library service?

Do we need to miniaturize recorded information to any greater reduction ratio than is now possible? (For the past several decades, area-reduction factors of five hundred to one or so have been feasible, and if fully exploited this alone would, in principle, permit one to reduce libraries to office size. Why, therefore, has it not come about? Is there too much interest in seeking ultra-high ratios? Optical microscopy offers million-to-one area reduction. Richard Feynman, a noted physicist, has drawn attention to the staggering thought that electron microscopy, at

---

[2] Don Swanson, "Dialogues with a Catalog," *Library Quarterly*, XXXIV (January, 1964), 113–25.

ten-billion-to-one area reduction, in principle, permits one thousand books to be put on the head of a pin—or all the world's recorded knowledge on one page.)

What are the implications for library education of advanced computer technology and of miniaturization applied to future libraries and information centers?

Should the planners and designers of future libraries receive a different kind of education from those who will operate future libraries?

Is it practical to ask that a library system keep track of what its users have requested so that the user can ask more easily for what he has seen once?

Can a library system be designed to adapt itself better in the course of time to the requirements of its users?

Can the benefits of sound systems planning accrue even to those who cannot afford automation?

INTELLECTUAL ACCESS TO INFORMATION

Indexing, subject analysis, reference, bibliography, classification, and cataloging all deal with the conceptual problems of gaining intellectual access to information. The intellectual aspects of these tasks can perhaps be most clearly distinguished from the vocational aspects by considering their design rather than their application. The study of formal rules of indexing, so that one can appreciate both the limitations and capabilities of machines for performing these tasks, must clearly be a part of library education. In related studies of semantics, syntax, thesaurus compilation, generics, search strategy, and theories of file storage and organization, one can recognize important mathematical and linguistic problems. In some respects these problems overlap problems of systems planning and analysis, but the overlap itself is less important than is recognition of the inherent mathematical and scientific content of this area of librarianship.

What are the intellectual processes and what are the mechanistic processes involved in indexing and classification? What is the detailed structure of the reference dialogue between the user and the library system?

What purpose does "browsing" serve, and must it necessarily take place in the stacks?

What are the common attributes and what are the important differences among the numerous existing indexing, subject heading, and classification systems?

How effective are present libraries and information systems in producing relevant information in response to subject-oriented requests for information?

What are the inherent logical problems involved in dealing with the notion of the "relevance" of a book or an article to a request for information on a subject?

In what areas and to what extent do we need increased subject control "in-depth" over recorded information?

How does retrieval effectiveness vary with the depth of indexing?

If techniques of ultra-miniaturization could put the world's store of recorded knowledge on a single page, or even in our desk drawer, what would be the fundamental significance, if any, of such a capability?

What level of subject knowledge is

required of those who index, classify, or provide reference assistance?

Does the role of classification in human mental processes justify studying the latter as part of library science?

What elements are common to the various subject specialties of special librarianship?

To what extent can the librarian be bypassed in putting the user of recorded knowledge into more direct contact with that knowledge?

What new and useful kinds of intellectual access to information can be envisioned?

DEVELOPMENT OF BOOK COLLECTIONS

Library education must take into account the intellectual, conceptual, and engineering problems involved in creating a collection of books adapted to the purposes that it is intended to serve. Again, these intellectual problems can perhaps best be recognized by considering the design of book-selection aids rather than their application and use by librarians. Insofar as library users might be provided with access to books other than those in a collection immediately at hand, we are led to consider problems of the optimal allocation of limited resources. The expense of delivering books from a remote point competes with cost of acquisition in a local collection. Book selection and acquisition thus become related to systems analysis. Here we must ask more seriously the extent to which knowledge of books is an essential prerequisite to skilful acquisitions librarianship.

What criteria can be used to measure the quality of a book collection?

In what way can the accessibility of other nearby or distant collections be taken into account in establishing criteria for acquisitions?

Should the bibliographic tools of the collection go well beyond the boundaries of the collection itself, and what should be the detailed relationship between the two?

What different kinds of libraries and library purposes must be recognized as particularly relevant to the process of book-selection?

Assuming that direct and personal knowledge of all books in a collection is far beyond the capabilities of any single librarian, what external resources should be exploited in the development of a collection?

To what extent should the acquisition and selection process assume the obligation of quality judgment?

Is not the weeding of obsolete materials as much a process of collection development as is selection and acquisition?

Should a library-school curriculum include courses on book selection?

THE CONFERENCE SPEAKERS

The contributors to this conference have been selected not because of their wide experience in librarianship but because each brings an important perspective to library education to which the profession would do well to pay heed. These perspectives cover a wide range of opinions and offer virtually unlimited opportunity for debate and controversy. Whether librarians should be essentially literate scholars with a pervasive knowledge of books, or "numerate" information technologists with good understanding of computing machines can be expected to typify the issues that arise. Selected viewpoints of philosophy, sociology, mathematics, engineering, classification, bookmanship, librarianship, documentation, information retrieval, and information science are represented in this conference. We took a calculated risk of ending up with more answers than there are questions. This introduction has thus attempted to equalize any such imbalance by providing a supply of questions, and, at the same time, hopefully placing its audience in a critical frame of mind.

The diverse and unusual background of each of our speakers prevents their being introduced as belonging to some easily identifiable niche, category, or pigeonhole. I know that they share one particularly important attribute—they are all well worth hearing on almost any subject. I can think of no more fitting introduction to any one of them than the story of the eccentric scientists who managed somehow to breed a strange and wonderful creature by crossing a parrot with a tiger. In reply to many questions on the nature of the beast they could only say, "We don't know much about it yet, but when it speaks—we listen!"

THE AGE OF THE SYMBOL—A PHILOSOPHY OF LIBRARY EDUCATION

ABRAHAM KAPLAN

THE business of philosophy, as I see it, is not to provide answers for other people's questions, and certainly not to make virtual decisions on their behalf without being willing to shoulder the responsibility that goes along with the power to make decisions. To my mind, the role of philosophy is, like art, to hold the mirror up to nature, and particularly to hold the mirror up to human nature—more especially, to human nature in its more confused and miserable moments. So what I intend to do is to restate the problems of which, I think, you are all very well aware but to put these problems in a broader perspective than that in which you ordinarily see them. I hope also that hearing these problems put by someone altogether removed from your profession and having them more fully articulated in this broad perspective may make it easier, if not to solve the problems, at least to continue to live with them.

So far as I am aware, librarianship is really in a critical condition—critical not just in terms of the enormous excess of demand over supply with regard to the performance of your function, but critical in a more basic respect. As it appears from the outside, the profession itself is now unsure of what its functions are and unsure also of just how to go about performing whatever functions are assigned to it or that it adopts. This state of affairs seems to me to be entirely understandable in the light of certain developments that affect not merely the profession but our society as a whole.

THE AGE OF THE SYMBOL

Specifically, enormous changes at every level of modern society can be associated with the concept of *information*. First, there is the sheer volume of information with which our society now must deal. The explosion of knowledge may be more familiar to this special group than the other much more widely publicized population explosion. In any event I venture to say that the knowledge explosion, even though it is not so widely recognized and attended to as a social problem in the way the population explosion is, in the long run may present the more serious difficulties and correspondingly open up the more challenging opportunities. I had occasion to estimate a few years ago that the number of printed words (setting aside all other media by which information is transmitted) produced annually in the United States amount to approximately ten million for each man, woman, and child. Or again the really dramatic statistic has now been widely disseminated that something on the order of 95 per cent of all the scientists who have ever lived are alive today—however broadly one chooses to define "scientist." No doubt symbols in their various forms and media occupy a larger part in our lives today than ever before, and the size of that part (if I may so express it) is growing exponentially.

At the same time that information

itself has this tremendous impact, theories about information, or more generally, theories about symbol processes, exert a similar force. From the standpoint of the theory of ideas, at any rate, if not from a broader social or cultural point of view, there would be good reason to propose still another general characterization of our age. Ours is the age of the *symbol*. It is really quite extraordinary how many intellectual disciplines either have come into being around processes of symbolization or have begun to focus about the nature of language and symbolism. This is apparent in philosophy, aesthetics, linguistics, psychoanalysis, political science—and the list can be extended quite far.

In the third place, co-ordinate with the growth of the symbol itself and the increasing importance in a variety of directions of theories of its working, there has also been a fantastic growth in the technology by which information is produced, processed, and transmitted. Computers, for instance, I have recently been told, have, during the course of the past quarter century or so, been growing by two orders of magnitude (i.e., a factor of 100) every five years, which is an extraordinary rate of growth—a rate having just the sort of fantastic quality that Don Swanson communicated to us with respect to the potentialities of miniaturization.

In this situation of rapid and tremendous change, it seems to me altogether understandable that a profession occupied centrally with precisely what underlies all these changes should find itself engaged in a search for some fixities in this flux, and concerned with re-examining the means that are available for the achievement of its purposes. I am saying first, then, that the problem of the profession is indeed a genuine problem and is a piece with a comparable problem which is being faced by many other professions, many other disciplines and, perhaps in a fundamental way, by our society as a whole. I now propose to discuss more specifically, against the background of this social change, what the nature and role of a library looks like from the outside, considered in the broadest possible terms. Only after some specification has been made of this can we speak sensibly of the nature and role of the educational process that is to train the profession for the management of the library.

I want to begin by restating one of Swanson's axioms, that what the library does or is to do depends upon the people for whom it is doing it. Everything in the library must ultimately be related to its uses, and these uses in turn must ultimately be dependent upon the users. Words do not mean anything, *people* mean things by words. Information means nothing, but *people* are informed and then take informed action or make informed decisions. And it seems to me important as a corollary of this axiom to recognize that the users and the uses can only be inductively determined. They are many and various and cannot be antecedently limited, except as a conjecture or prediction of what will be expected of us on some future occasion. But to say it is inductive is not to say that we cannot make any generalizations, that we dare not venture to predict, so I want to make some very general characterizations of what sorts of functions libraries have performed in the past and presumably will continue to perform in the future.

THE LIBRARY'S FUNCTION IN SOCIETY

I believe that what is most fundamentally constitutive of human culture, as distinct from various subhuman societies, however complex, is this: a society has a culture when the members of the society do not begin the process of learning from scratch with each generation, whenever (that is to say) it becomes possible for the society not to make the same mistakes too often. It is surely too much to expect any generation to begin where the preceding generation left off, but when it becomes possible at least to begin at a later point than the preceding generation began, then I think we can speak meaningfully of that society's having a culture. The library is for society what memory is for the individual, the repository of what has already been learned, including what has been badly learned or mislearned. At any rate it is the repository of past experience which is now available to be drawn upon in a present response. Admittedly the value of such a repository has, on occasion, been questioned. In Shaw's *Caesar and Cleopatra,* the library of Alexandria bursts into flames and Theodotus dashes in and pleads with Caesar for men and equipment to save it. "What is burning there," he says, "is the memory of mankind." Caesar, being an author, is not impressed. He responds, "A shameful memory. Let it burn." In specific cases, attitudes of this kind may be understandable, but that attitude cannot be generalized without abandoning our human status altogether. I venture to express my opinion that there are people, institutions, and forces at work in the world today which make precisely for this abandonment of the human status, because of the attacks which they mount, both directly and indirectly, against ideas, their expression, and their storage for subsequent effective use. A library, then, is first of all an archive, a repository in which society can find what it has already learned. This is also the earliest historical function of the institution, so far as a layman like me is acquainted with it.

There is a second kind of function which became particularly important in the United States around the turn of the century; in various ways I expect it will become more important in the emerging future. The library is a means of education, an instrumentality by which special groups and classes in the society can take advantage of experiences not directly their own, and so improve their position in society. In the past the public libraries of New York City and the other large American cities have rendered great services to immigrant and other minority populations. Under changing social circumstances, this can still be seen in forms varying according to the local conditions. I remember how struck I was some years ago, when I dropped into the local branch of the public library in West Los Angeles, to see how largely it was occupied by Americans of Japanese descent, for whom the library—and education—had become an important device by which they could be integrated into the American culture and find opportunity to fulfil their potentialities. I expect that in coming decades the library will have a notably important function to perform with respect to the Negro minority in the United States.

From a broad social standpoint, I

am not sure but what functions of this character are among the most important which libraries can perform. So long as we keep to the level of abstract generality and speak only of the growth of human knowledge and the ways in which systems of access to and processing of information can contribute to the growth of human knowledge, we are likely to overlook the socially fundamental fact that human knowledge is something which is known to very, very few human beings. Only one American out of twenty has had a college education, and I think in all candor we can admit that even a college education does not amount to so very much. Americans lag far behind other Western nations in the proportion of book readers (using even the most liberal definition of a book) in the population, in spite of a higher proportion of college graduates. Some years ago I was asked to testify in the trial of Henry Miller's *Tropic of Cancer* in California. It was a jury trial; I testified for the defense (which incidentally lost its case). The jury, it became apparent to me even in the short time that I participated in the trial, was not particularly of literate bent. I commented on this fact to the defense attorney and asked him how he ever had allowed himself to be saddled with a jury that so obviously was uninterested in books of any kind. All he could say was, "You should have seen the ones that got away." I say this not to derogate the jury system or the qualities and potentialities of the American people, or in the very least to reinforce any invidious distinction between an educated elite and an illiterate mass. Indeed, my intention is exactly the contrary. It is precisely because I want to break down —in every respect and wherever it appears—any such invidious distinction, that it seems to me we must recognize here a great social responsibility with respect to the functions to be performed by those who have authority and control over repositories of information.

There is a third general and basic function of the library: as an instrument of research. In terms of significant growth, this function is perhaps the most recent; it can be expected to become increasingly significant in the emerging future. Now, I mean research in its genuine sense. I do not want to legislate about meanings of words, but I do want to point out that the term "research," which is certainly one of the "O.K. words" of our time, is very widely used to mean nothing other than literally a re-search—that is to say, not an extension of the domain of knowledge but the making available to particular people some things that were already known but not specifically known to them at that time. The library is expected to be the primary instrument for making such "research" possible. There *are* certain functions of this kind to be performed, and it is not my intention to derogate them. It is only that I think we ought to call things by their right names.

What I am concerned about is the way in which knowledge already available can most effectively be put to such use as to increase the knowledge that is available. Indeed, this process of increase can take place only on the basis of knowledge available. I want to emphasize that a command of what has already been discovered is a necessary condition for making further discoveries. There is a danger here that the necessary condition might be mistaken for a sufficient condition. There is no doubt that a great many people look increasingly upon the librarian as the magic helper, and they believe everything that is needed could be provided if only there were properly designed and operated systems in libraries. But they overlook the fact that discovery is still a creative effort in which the researcher himself has certain significant responsibilities. The sort of thing that may happen is quite comparable to a situation that recurrently poses problems in the field of psychoanalysis, where the patient comes to expect that the therapist will do whatever need be done to improve the patient's situation, while he himself can be absolved of any responsibility. There is an additional danger, that after hearing over and over again from the patient how wonderful the therapist is, and how capable he is, if only he were willing to do all these things, the therapist comes to believe it. This is called countertransference; I suggest that some of the problems of your profession may be due in some measure, at any rate, to this countertransference, to the continued demands that are being made upon your profession by others as a way for them to get out from under their own responsibilities.

LIBRARY EDUCATION

It is not that I do not see any need for improvements in libraries or in the conduct of the profession, but I think also that we ought realistically to recognize the limits of what is sensibly to be assigned as a performance characteristic of an optimal system. Nevertheless, it is in terms of its serviceability as an instrument of research that I think what you are engaged in will probably be most important to users in the next years, and specifically for this reason. It is often remarked that as the frontiers of knowledge recede farther and farther toward the horizon, it takes longer and longer to traverse the domain until we reach the frontiers so that we can extend them. The history of the graduate school in general is a case in point, and I am sure you are finding it true, by the way, with regard to your own profession. I would conjecture that if, by the end of the conference, you were to come to agreement on the sorts of things that ought to be done in library school education, you would find that you needed three years or five years or seven, and every field faces these same kinds of pressures. The predictions have even been made that the progress of scientific inquiry is going to be slowed down and perhaps eventually choked off altogether, simply because human life is not long enough to allow anybody to master all that he needs to know in order to be able to make a new discovery.

Fortunately, as with various other dire predictions of this Malthusian kind, based on rates of growth and so on, there is another factor in the situation. That is that there are also, in part as a result of this very growth, remarkable advances in what we might call semantic transportation. There are faster ways to get out to this new frontier than previously available, and this, it seems to me, is one of the great and pressing tasks which your profession must increasingly come to grips with. The challenge is to maintain the flow of ideas; or let me say it is to transform the image of your profession, if I may so put it, from that of operating service stations in this flow of ideas, to being rather traffic and transportation engineers, where the problems of the flow are dealt with from a large-scale and fundamental point of view. It is something like the change, if not in the image, certainly increasingly in the actual practice, of the medical profession, where it is no longer a matter of sitting and waiting for the patient to come to be treated for a particular illness but where increasingly the profession is occupied with preventive medicine and with participating in the working of decisions that will directly affect the public health.

HUMANISTIC BASIS OF LIBRARY EDUCATION

What I want to do is spell out some of the implications that I see in this general perspective of the functions of the library and some of the implications for education in the profession of librarians. It seems to me clear, first of all, that the humanistic basis is there and will and must remain as a basis, provided that "humanistic" is conceived in ways that do not prejudice it as belonging to one of two antithetical cultures. (Having been trained as a chemist as an undergraduate and finding myself nowadays occupied almost entirely with matters like religion and art and politics, I have never had very much sympathy for this whole thesis of "the two cultures." At any rate, I certainly see nothing necessary in the dualism by which it is so often preconceived.) Surely knowledge of the uses, and therefore, of the users of information, must always remain fundamental. That is nothing other than knowledge of people and of the various things that people do and of the various ways in which in the course of those doings they generate and transmit and interpret ideas or information. I would suppose then that sometime in the course of training, whether as an undergraduate or in the graduate library school itself, the student will have been exposed to something of the sociology of knowledge, to something of the history of ideas, and to something of the structure of inquiry, not merely in some area that might happen to be of special interest to him but in broad historical and cultural terms.

But I want to go farther. It seems to me that this humanistic basis includes not only a certain appropriate set of beliefs about what men are like and what they are up to, and how they make use of ideas, but also a certain appropriate set of values. It seems to me that every profession, if it is to be meaningful, at least to its practitioners, must always be something of a calling, something to which we are impelled from within, that is—literally a vocation and not merely an occupation. I would think that an inculcation of the love of learning, of the love of ideas, of the love of truth, and even of the love of books, is an entirely appropriate part of the training in this profession. I recently encountered the reports of some studies that have been made in various medical schools of the attitudes of students on a variety of value questions pertaining to the conduct of the medical profession. Roughly speaking, the findings were to this effect: that among first-year students in medical schools there is a great deal of moral idealism with respect to the practice of medicine, and this steadily declines and reaches its lowest point when the student has completed his medical training. This is very rightfully giving great cause for concern to medical school educators. Of course I do not mean to imply for one moment that there are any comparable phenomena in library schools; but I do suggest that you might be well advised to face this possibility and to incorporate in your curriculums or other programs some devices intended to ward off the danger, even if it is not recognized now.

For example, it seems to me quite clear that there is a certain kind of social responsibility that is involved in resisting the pressures of various interest groups and institutions or social conditions in which you operate, which interfere with the proper discharge of your functions. I believe that the profession itself has a responsibility to stand up against those pressures and not to assume that it is somebody else that must protect the profession. I do not mean to say that it is your sole responsibility, but I do imply that you cannot altogether be absolved of it and that your training, therefore, ought to make it possible for you to recognize and discharge that kind of responsibility.

VOCATIONAL EDUCATION

Second, in addition to this humanistic basis, as I have called it, there are certainly some specific vocational elements, as Don Swanson put them, in matters of learning *how,* and not merely learning *that* such and such is the case. There is no particular problem with these, except possibly the following which I would mention by way of anticipation. It is not to be supposed that suitably designed systems and appropriately selected computer or other automatic devices will lessen the demands that are being made on knowing "how," rather than knowing "that." On the contrary, if anything, they will intensify those demands. Here, for once, is a place where I think philosophy is in a position to say something definitive. This point was first made explicitly, to my knowledge, at the end of the eighteenth century by Immanuel Kant, who was discussing the relationship between the faculty of judgment, which is the faculty of relating general principles to particular cases, and the faculties of understanding and of reason which operate to produce and combine these general principles. Kant made the point that the faculty of judgment is absolutely indispensable and always will be, because even if rules can be provided to specify under what conditions a principle should be applied to a particular case, judgment is still called for to apply the rules to the cases they govern. There will always be a need, therefore, for these sorts of skills, though their specific content will, of course, change as the instrumentalities with which they operate change.

THE MATHEMATICAL SCIENCES AS A BASIS FOR LIBRARY EDUCATION

The heart of the whole problem, as I encounter it from the outside, relates to a third general area, what the conference refers to as the intellectual foundation of library science. As to this, coming with my particular preconceptions (maybe prejudices, prejudgments), I see no alternative but to recognize that this intellectual foundation can be provided by nothing other than the whole set of disciplines which I lump together under the name of "metasciences." These are sciences not about subject matters provided by man and nature, but about subject matters provided fundamentally by our ideas *about* man and nature, or by our language, or by our ways of transmitting and processing the information that we have derived, and so on. I mean disciplines like mathematics, logic, linguistics, semantics, and, in the narrower sense, theory of information, and maybe cybernetics. These disciplines then range off into other related metasciences. I say that these are fundamental because it seems to me that the only alternative to these (taken all together and without concern over points of detail) as a foundation for the professional studies would be a narrow specialism or a really quite impossible encyclopedism. There may have been a time in earlier generations when it could be expected that the librarian would know all there is to know, and the measure of his effectiveness in the discharge of his function could have been provided to a significant degree by the measure of how completely he had mastered human knowledge and interests. This, it seems to me, is a possibility that has forever vanished. Or on the other side, a narrow specialism in which one is concerned only with a particular subject ("I'm going to learn *that; that's* my foundation, and the rest is a matter of applying some tricks of the trade") —this, it seems to me, would fail dismally to perform any of the general functions that I tried to sketch earlier.

I could give some specific examples of the ways in which even disciplines like metaphysics or the history of philosophy have an impact on some of your basic concerns, especially those connected with classification, intellectual access to materials, and so on. From the little acquaintance that I have with these concerns, I am struck by the extent to which many are victimized by what Edward Sapir and in more recent times Benjamin Lee Whorf identified as the myth of a "natural logic." This is the supposition that there are certain ways in which we *must* think about things, certain lines along which the world *must* be conceived of as articulated. For Sapir and Whorf these are a function to a significant degree of the basic structure of the language which we employ in marking out the discriminations in the world; from other philosophical points of view they might be connected with various metaphysics to which we subscribe. At any rate, the so-called problem of the Categories, for example, has been an important problem for philosophy, not only in Western culture, but in Indian and Chinese philosophy as well, for many, many centuries. I would suppose this problem is also relevant to the organization of a library.

But I take it that it is really not this which is the most pressing, or at any rate, the most hotly debated issue in your field today. That, I suppose, beyond question, concerns automation. I should like, then, to make a few remarks about how these developments seem to me to bear upon library education.

First, I insisted earlier that the intellectual foundation for library science must be fundamentally this group of metasciences—logic, linguistics, mathematics, theory of information, and so on. Now I believe that they have this centrality, not because they underlie the new computer technology or related technologies like miniaturization, but for an intellectual reason, because there is central to them the concept of structure, of order, of form, which seems to me to be precisely the central concern also of library science. I am unable to conceptualize any alternative. Either you are interested in order, structure, form, or you are interested in substance and content; and, in the latter case, you must resign yourself to mastering some increasingly narrow subject area and to doing whatever you can in the course of that work as little assistants or magic helpers or something of the kind to the people working in the area.

Although fundamentally, I think, it is in intellectual terms that these disciplines become important, they also may become important in a secondary way through technology, for, after all, it is form and structure that lie at the basis of both computer design and application.

I believe quite generally that technology is not a threat to humanistic values. Quite the contrary, technology is liberating—at any rate in its potentialities. (No one would be such a fool, or so blind to actualities, as to say that it is always liberating in fact.) But so much of what I hear expressed and what I sense to be felt though unexpressed about the threat of the new technology impresses me as subject to one serious, indeed, fatal blunder. People talk as though Frankenstein were the name of the monster and not the name of the man who built the monster. We do indeed have good reason to be apprehensive about Frankenstein, but the object of that apprehension lies ultimately within ourselves, or at any rate, within the human beings who are making use of technologies in one direction or another.

THE LAW OF THE INSTRUMENT

On the other hand, I find often operative—very widely, for instance, in the conduct of the behavioral sciences—a very human and very understandable tendency (but no less objectionable for being understood) to do the things that we already know how to do. We tend to formulate our problems in such a way as to make it seem that the solutions to those problems demand precisely what we already happen to have at hand. With respect to the conduct of inquiry, and especially in behavioral science, I label this effect "the law of the instrument." The simplest formulation I know of the law of the instrument runs this way: give a small boy a hammer and it will turn out that everything he encounters needs pounding.

Now the law of the instrument I think is operative, not only spuriously on *behalf* of automation, but also and equally spuriously *against* it. It seems to me that people very often allow their attitudes toward the use of various kinds of automated systems and devices to be determined, not by a realistic assessment of the needs and the ways in which these needs can be met most effectively with the means available, but rather by the determination that it has to be these means. The means themselves predetermine what we are to do. Or there is at work a converse determination: "That's one thing I'm *not* going to use; I know it won't work and I'll have nothing to do with it." When both of these points of view are set aside, it seems to me that one can recognize certain potentialities which, for my part, I confidently expect will be increasingly actualized by and large for an incomparably more effective performance of the humanistic function.

SIMILARITY BETWEEN PHILOSOPHY AND LIBRARIANSHIP

There is one other thing that I think I can say with respect to your problem that may be of help, possibly of more help than anything I have said to this point. Very often we like to talk over our problems with somebody else, or to hear somebody else discuss them, because it comes as such a sense of relief to discover that other people have the same problems, and that these are even worse, perhaps, for them. I want to take just a moment or two to point out that the problem in philosophy is really not very dissimilar, so far as I can see. There are many points of kinship. Like your profession, mine also has thrust upon it, as its appropriate domain, the whole of knowledge, the whole of culture; nothing is supposed to be foreign to us, and we ought to be prepared under suitable circumstances to be helpful with regard to any and every area of human concern. Like you, we cannot even begin to occupy ourselves with the substance and content of this endless domain, but only with its form, with its structure, with its order, with the interrelations of the various parts. Like you also, our problems always come to us from outside our profession, unless indeed, we are content, as I am afraid many members of my profession are, just to chew our own entrails—to make a living by taking in each other's washing. What is worse is not only that our problems come to us from outside the profession, but that the adequacy of our treatment of the problems is also judged outside the profession, and we remain eternally middlemen.

That is our common problem; the point at which we meet is most poignantly and most effectively expressed by that great philosopher of our time, Charlie Brown. Charlie Brown is talking to Linus, who has just taken out a library card and who is really very much distressed about the whole experience, and Charlie is being reassuring. He says, "I think I can understand your fear of libraries, Linus. Library fever is similar to other mental disturbances. You fear the library rooms because they are strange to you. You are out of place. All of us have certain areas in which we feel out of place."

"Oh," says Linus, "in what area do you feel out of place, Charlie Brown?"

"Earth."

THE STUDY OF THE USE AND USERS OF RECORDED KNOWLEDGE[1]

PHILIP H. ENNIS

THE word "knowledge" in the title of this paper will gradually transmute to the word "information," because the emphasis of this conference is on professional and scientific uses of knowledge and the word "information" is associatively more at home in this context. It is important, however, to note that man's printed record carries other associations; moral instruction and sustenance, imaginative release and recreation, individual and social solace and satire. The use and users of these aspects of recorded knowledge have not as yet been studied as intensively as have "information users"; they should not be forgotten, however.

Before we can discuss how to *study* use and users, some boundaries and distinctions are necessary. Otherwise practically all of library science could be subsumed into this field, which is large and untidy enough. The first distinction is a cautionary note for us not to fall into a total concern with the needs of the present users of libraries, for the classical responsibility of the library to collect and preserve a body of recorded materials implies that the future users should be considered. Since their needs are likely to be different from those of the present users, flexibility of all library functions is imperative.

Next, two apparently fragmentary ancedotes introduce a tentative architecture for this area of user studies.

The first story is about a scientist friend of mine who was talking with me about books and reading. He observed, in a moment of self-discovery, that his professional reading was quite different from his recreational reading. For the latter he read in the traditional way, from the beginning through to the end. In his professional reading, however, he often read backward, turning first to the conclusions of an article, then working back to the data, then finally back to the introductory statement of the problem. I have done this myself and recognized immediately the differences in these two ways of reading. It is not entirely or simply a matter of speed, but different purposes are being served.

The second story is the paradox that, at the same time great sums of money are being spent to develop more efficient abstracting services which condense information into short bundles, the *New York Review of Books* has become a considerable success—and its most outstanding feature is the *long* review.

Both these observations point to a decisive distinction between *general* audiences for books on the one hand and *specialized* audiences for particular types of recorded information on the other. The general audience is comprised of an unknown number of individuals, scattered invisibly across the entire landscape of the country. Their reading serves a variety of purposes and is comprised of many disparate patterns.

---

[1] I am indebted to Carol Woolpy for her help in organizing and tabulating the quantitative parts of this paper.

In contradistinction, the audiences for specialized communication can generally be bounded by familiar occupational or institutional labels, within the scientific communities, the medicine and health field, education, engineering, and so forth. There are other kinds of specialized audiences as well, those, for example, defined by religious or ethnic boundaries or those created by specialized leisure interests.

TABLE 1

SCHEMATIC ARCHITECTURE OF USE STUDIES

PERSPECTIVE OF STUDY	TYPE OF AUDIENCE	
	General	Specialized
"Inside" the library	1	2
"Outside" the library	3	4

There are a multiplicity of general audiences and a multiplicity of specialized audiences which overlap within and between each other in an unraveled tangle. Nevertheless, the *conceptual* separation of the two types, though certainly not new, is vital, for the two types of audience invite a different kind of question, each of which in turn relates to a different and basic sociological problem.

A second distinction, of comparable importance, is that which differentiates research primarily oriented to problems *inside* the library from those concerned mainly with those *outside* or beyond the library. Researches "inside" the library deal with problems of contact between users and a library function, be it acquisition, reference service, the use of the catalog, or circulation. Studies "outside" the libraries have to do with the broader issues of identifying the characteristics of readers, describing their communications practices, and sources of information, including the library as but one source among many.

If we put these two dimensions together, we have four basic types of user studies, shown in Table 1.

It should be clear that these four kinds of studies do not specify anything about methods of research, types of libraries, or sources of data. In fact, a variety of libraries, methods, and data is used in each of the four kinds of studies. I am not sure that all of the many kinds of studies of library use and users can be fitted into this scheme, but a surprisingly large number do. To illustrate the kinds of studies that fall in each of the cells, cell 1, the studies of general audiences inside the library, would contain research into catalog use, or analyses of reference questions. In cell 2 are studies which describe how specialists of one kind or other (e.g., physicians, engineers, scientists, or scholars) use various library services or facilities. In cell 3 are the familiar studies which ask who is reading what kinds of books and where do they come from, and in cell 4 are several different kinds of studies, the most familiar type being the study, through interview, diary, or observation, aimed at describing the communications patterns and information needs of different kinds of specialists. It is these latter studies that have, I think, most often been called "use or user" studies. At least two other kinds of studies also fall into cell 4; they are, first, "readership studies" wherein the specialist's response to a particular publication is analyzed, and, second, citation studies, in which specialist journals, typically in some field of science, are analyzed for the references cited in their articles. Later I will have more to say about the distribution of studies in these cells and about user-research problems generally.

For most of the paper, however, I would like to discuss this fourfold table, identify its intellectual roots, and draw some implications for the study of the use of recorded knowledge.

First, let us consider the distinction between general and specialized audiences. As noted above, each has generated a typical kind of question which, in turn, has shaped its research traditions. For general audiences the studies have been designed mainly to arm librarians, educators, and publishers in the perennial struggle to create and maintain an adult audience of readers. A key element in that struggle was the instilling and sustaining of motivation to read. Thus, a good deal of inquiry was devoted to discovering the techniques to get people to read and to evaluating the efficacy of those techniques.

For specialized audiences, on the other hand, motivation to read has been pretty much taken for granted. It is assumed that a specialized audience, in seeking information, is carrying out some well-motivated performance of an occupational role, for example, scientist, physician. Being informed and keeping up with the literature are part of that role.

The basic problem of the specialized audience, instead, becomes a diffusion-decision problem—that is, a description of the communication structure of a specialized audience, a tracing of recorded messages proceeding through that structure, and an evaluation of the impact of these messages on the decisions that are made in the course of performing the specialized functions of the particular audience.

There is another way to describe the difference between a general and a special audience. It is in the relations—quantitative and qualitative—between their readers and writers. Quantitatively, the difference may be described in terms of the ratio of writers to readers. One can define the degree of specialization of an audience partly by its absolute size and partly by the extent to which the number of writers approaches the number of readers.

Qualitatively, the difference between a general and a special audience is the kind and amount of feed-back from reader to writer. In the special audience there is more of the tendency for a member to be, at alternate times, reader *and* writer, with the channel of recorded knowledge being part of mutual communication. In the general audience the reader simply tends to say yea or nay (accept or reject), to various items transmitted. In brief this is the difference between two-way communication and one-way communication. This means one- or two-way communication thru that channel only. The exchange of money for words indicates that there are feed-back processes in general audiences as well, but they are different and have different consequences for the system. And above all, they involve the librarian in different ways for each system.

So to continue the logic of the previously mentioned fourfold table, it should be noted that the research question asked of each type of audience can be answered either from the point of view of the *library's contribution* or from the point of view of the *audience as a whole*.

Now these two different ways of formulating problems have historically grown from the library's practical concerns and from its professional ideology, some key elements of which are to serve everyone and to educate as you serve. Most professions generate such research perspectives in the same way, yet they vary in the extent to which their everyday practice and research are related to the intellectual apparatus of basic research, carried on by the more traditional university line departments. Part of that intellectual apparatus is research methodology. It seems clear that librarianship has borrowed liberally and creatively from the variety of methods developed by the social sciences. The incorporation of social science theories, concepts, and ideas into library science, however, has not seemed to me to have gone very far. Perhaps it is the tradition of polemical reassertion of library ideology mixed with a constricting pragmatism that prevents a cumulating body of theory. I mean here particularly the reliance on local surveys to match ALA standards.

Yet it seems imperative and possible to move in this direction, for the two formulations of the problems mentioned above suggest a translation of user studies into broad sociological concepts, furnishing thereby an abundant and continuing resource of ideas and empirical generalizations. To illustrate, the problem of making and keeping an adult audience for books is an example of the generic question as to how any habit, taste, or preference is maintained as a voluntary choice in a competitive and pluralistic society. The social process of creating and sustaining buttermilk-drinkers, bowlers, Republican voters, Beethoven-lovers, and book-readers is similar and in some cases identical.

While there is no single or definitive answer to the generic question of how tastes are formed and maintained, the processes of socialization and the processes of persuasion are the two most obvious and probably critical involved in creating and securing an audience for anything. That is, many tastes and preferences are either directly or indirectly created in the early school years; surely reading is one of these. So it is an important part of any research program on general reading to explore the array and relative strength of the influences determining skill and motivation to read all through the early years, especially at critical transition points in a child's development. Similarly, the preservation of reading as an adult habit requires the same kind of treatment. There are important clues that reading, like many other minority tastes in American life, depends upon some degree of social support for the activity, over and above the intrinsic satisfaction that the act of reading gives. Informal social support from family and friends, and more formal efforts at persuasion and influence, as well as the whole study of socialization, have a rich research tradition in modern psychology and sociology.

An analogous translation can be made with the librarian's concern for the diffusion of information and its use among specialized groups. This formulation of the problem derives from one of the most important structural facts of modern industrialized societies, namely, the traditional professions (law and medicine), many of the maturing professions (architecture, teaching, social work, nursing, librarianship), many occupations even further removed from the professional niche (such as city planner, computer programmer, traffic engineer), and finally even occupations as farmer, skilled machine craftsmen, and sports instructors—all are increasingly dependent on basic research done in traditional departments of universities, special research institutions, and industrial and governmental laboratories. The physical, life, earth, and behavioral sciences transmit their research results through a dense tangle of special interest groups and occupational specialities via a communications network including formal conferences and meetings, journals of every type and level, and a variety of informal channels ranging from letters to corridor chats.

There are several social-science areas dealing directly with these problems, all of which can contribute basic intellectual resources for library science. The sociology of science, a rapidly growing subspecialty in the field, is an important one, the modern counterparts of communications research is another, and the interdisciplinary field of organization theory is still a third.

At this point, the obvious solution to both the curriculum problem and the research problem involved in studying library users would be to have those students interested in public libraries and work with children and young people take those social-science courses that deal with the processes of socialization and persuasion. Those students interested in special libraries and research libraries can be directed into courses in the sociology of science, organizational theory, and so forth. This is, I suppose, what is done now insofar as the social sciences enter the library-school curriculum at all. And if such practices were extended, all to the good.

But suppose we reverse the questions and ask about the communications patterns in a general audience and its relation to their decisions. Conversely, suppose we ask how to create and maintain interests for specialized fields. Such an orientation seems difficult to carry through, especially when we examine the implicit premise of the two questions. For studies of specialized audiences the touchstone has been the logic of *efficiency:* knowledge of communications patterns and assessments of information services to specialists, evaluated by the yardstick of efficiency. This is possible because there are objective criteria of assessing the *effect* of various measures on productivity of the specialized audience, as measured by quantitative counts of articles or books or products produced or by individual or group judgments as to the usefulness of various bibliographic tools or other publications.

In contrast, a general audience can only report what it likes, how much of what kind of things it reads, and where it gets them. Since there is no consensus as to desired effects of general reading and no way of assessing whatever effects do occur, the question as to efficiency hardly seems appropriate. The only way the efficiency criterion has been used with respect to general audiences is with the ability of a library or any other agency to produce readers or circulation. Sheer amount of use and the degree of success in winning the non-reader become, therefore, the major services that tend to be measured quantitatively. The empirical studies of catalog use and reference service are among the weakest in all library research. Yet there may be gains in reversing the questions, especially if we shift associative gears somewhat. General audiences may not be a scattered and random aggregate of isolated individuals—the implicit assumption about them. There is, in fact, impressive evidence that such "general" audiences are constantly being moved in the direction of organization and specialization. Just a few items to show this pervasive tendency.

First, is the now-established finding (still new to some, however) that people come in groups: family, neighborhood, friendship, work, religious, ethnic, and so on. One of the elements of these groups is a division of function; some people sharpen the pencils and some people write with them. Another element is that some people initiate and sanction group activities, while others follow and support group action. The discovery of "opinion leader-ship" as a characteristic of large statistical aggregates of people bound together by community or ethnic ties provides a microstructure from which larger organized groupings emerge. And they emerge from the natural coagulative tendency for likes to seek out each other to share and to defend their interests. The process might begin and only go as far as, say, the Tall Girl Clubs that exist in practically all major metropolitan areas—they simply sponsor activities that will attract tall men and lobby among clothing and shoe manufacturers regarding the tall girl's special problems. In the field of reading we find comparably the Joyce Society, the Baker Street Irregulars, the now almost extinct but lamentably unstudied Browning Societies which once filled the landscape, or the countless book-review clubs formed by literate housewives. I wonder, incidentally, if these clubs have disappeared over the years or is it simply their relative invisibility to me, compared to my youth, when my mother would be all in a panic when it was her turn to give her book report. (It was not clear then, or now, whether it was the intellectual task of the book review or the social task of serving an elegant tea that caused the panic, or maintained the group.)

Such "natural" groupings are sometimes strengthened, sometimes initiated, by the possibility of commercial advantage. The obvious case is the systematic development of special-interest book clubs—the emphasis is rarely put on the word *club* as meaning an association. Bowker lists about one hundred of them, all captured by the familiar wisdom that when he is properly identified, it is a more predictable strategy to sell one man ten books than ten men one book. Finally and most puzzling is the more vaporous structuring of literature subpublics of various types.[2] Little is known of their boundaries, internal differentiation, and overlap.

The same approach, that is, seeing the group structure within the general audience, is applicable to young people as well as adults. For example, everyone has talked for years about the reading ladder. Get children on simple things, and gradually there will be a development of taste. This is, as far as I can see, empirically unsupported and will probably remain so long as teachers and librarians tear up every year, in the name of efficiency, all the records they should have been keeping for

[2] I recall here the insightful identification of this phenomenon by David Riesman in an article on reading in which he described the *New Yorker* cartoon about the young man who replied to the question whether he had read a current bestseller with the words, "Not personally."

longitudinal studies. Not only is the structuring of book choices among young people important, but also the social influences around them guiding the extent and nature of their reading. A pilot project Sara Fenwick and I are carrying out in a Chicago public school suggests that for sixth-graders reading patterns are very diverse but clearly linked to their immediate world. We had group interviews with five average youngsters, then later that week a group interview with their fathers, then an interview with the mothers, another session with the children and a final group interview with their current teacher, their librarian, and their teacher of the previous year. Taking this entire population as an interrelated system we found interesting areas of misperception—differing expectations as to who should be doing what about reading and learning. Mothers differed with the fathers; parents with teachers; and the children appeared immensely more knowledgeable about the attempted control procedures the adults used than I had supposed.

In short, it seems propitious to explore, once more, the structure of reading audiences, beginning perhaps with a study to describe the variety of reading habits. The admirable start made years ago by Ruth Strang, in her *Explorations in Reading Patterns*,[3] might very well be tried again with new tools and new concepts.

With respect to specialized audiences, the reversal of the traditional library-research question would produce, I believe, several different research directions. One is toward the level of specialized systems as a whole. Specifically, an important limitation of many user studies is that they have been generally restricted in scope, dealing largely with one specialized audience at a time. This makes good sense methodologically and is the right approach if the unit under study is the individual user. But if the scope of the inquiry is extended under the directive of the kind of question asked of general audiences, then the perspective would see specialized audiences themselves as subunits in a larger institutional sector. For example, in the field of public primary and secondary education there are literally hundreds of specialized audiences who have some share in the operation and decision-making of a city or a state's educational system. An even larger number of specialized sub-audiences comprises the health sector. Combined with the fact that increasing numbers of occupations are being guided by the findings of basic science, the increasing interrelations among and between specialized groups make it important to look at the diffusion patterns of larger systems, including their network of information centers, libraries, and whatever other dissemination channels there are.

The methodology for such extensive studies is still in its infancy, but one point seems clear; as the design of such communications-systems studies increases in scope, the likelihood that individual users will be the basic unit of inquiry will lessen.

A second direction of study of specialized audiences emerges when we now take as problematical the motivation of specialists, and ask not only what are they doing and what do they need, but what kinds of motivations—individual and socially prescribed—are involved. Such inquiries are especially important when focused on the mutual

---

[3] Ruth Strang, *Explorations in Reading Patterns* (Chicago: University of Chicago Press, 1942).

expectations of specialist and librarian. It is more than likely that there are mutual misperceptions and misunderstandings as to who should be doing what about the control of information dissemination. Moreover, there is likely to be in specialized fields a counterpart of a common librarian-patron difficulty in the general audience field. It is the familiar complaint that people hardly ever ask the question they really want to ask, but it takes the skills of the reference librarian in what might be called an information interview to bring out the real problem and then to prescribe the solution. Even on this level, the same is probably true for librarians dealing with specialists, but to a lesser extent, for they are often housed together in the same organization, and the reference librarian himself is likely to be somewhat of an expert on the particular specialty. A more important difficulty is the degree of disagreement as to the subject classification schemes and basic categories involved, as well as the social control over the use of various categories.

Such disagreements will probably become more serious as advanced information technology continues to reshuffle task allocations back and forth between the specialist and those in charge of packaging information and moving it from one place to another and from one person to another. For instance, this is the influential opinion of Alvin Weinberg:

> The later steps of the information transfer process, such as retrieval, are strongly affected by the attitudes and practices of the originators of scientific information. The working scientist must therefore share many of the burdens that have been traditionally carried by the professional documentalist. The technical community must devote a larger share than heretofore of its time and resources to the discriminating management of the ever-increasing technical record. Doing less will lead to fragmented and ineffective science and technology.[4]

And in almost direct contradiction is the advice of the recent report, *Toward the Library of the 21st Century:*

> The library itself will help the user find and organize textual material relevant to the subject he is studying... we know that certain advances already made or now envisioned in science hold promise of alleviating burdens of information usage in all activities that draw upon resources of the library.[5]

There are already some studies of specialized information moving in the direction of combining psychological-motivational variables with sociological level variables focused on the structure of the work group within which research is carried out.[6] It should be no surprise to learn that these kinds of studies originate outside the library world and indeed often outside the university community.

These examples indicate that, while the traditional presumptions lying behind the study of general or specific audiences for information are still not exhausted, reversing them produces some different and useful research suggestions. Such a reversal also makes it more difficult to design a curriculum. If general and specialized audiences

---

[4] Alvin Weinberg, "Scientific Communication," *International Science and Technology*, April, 1963, p. 65.

[5] Bolt, Beranek, and Newman, Inc., *Toward the Library of the 21st Century* (Cambridge, Mass.: Council on Library Resources, 1964), pp. 1, 10.

[6] See, e.g., the recent work, John A. Postley *et al.*, *Report on a Study of Behavioral Factors in Information Systems* (Los Angeles: Hughes Dynamics, n.d.); and the older investigations; Herbert A. Shepard, "The Value of a University Research Group," *American Sociological Review*, XIX (1954), 456–62.

should be examined from both sets of presumptions, and if, as is clearly the case, types of libraries do not coincide very well with the distinction between general versus specific, then one cannot simply send public and school librarians off to one set of social-science courses and special and academic-research librarians off to another set. There is no easy answer to this. One choice is to send all library students to a carefully and individually chosen set of courses in sociology, psychology, economics, and so on. The risks here are that they will not be absorbed in the routine research and teaching assistantships and important informal relationships in either their library school or the social-science departments. Moreover, these departments are oriented toward producing their own products and furthering their own research interests; this is likely to create, albeit inadvertently, even further exclusionary practices toward our visiting library students.

A second choice is to increase the number of specialists (social science or otherwise) on library-school faculties. The difficulty here, administrative and intellectual, is the potential isolation of the visiting faculty member rather than the student, and his inability to get library students interested in his research, which is tied to his parent discipline.

A third choice is to demand higher entrance requirements for students. Like all complex problems, experimentation with combinations of all three choices will have to be employed and will vary from school to school and from time to time. But if something is not done to reconnect the study of use and users to their intellectual roots in the social sciences, then the spasmodic and non-cumulative kind of library research will continue.

The amount and organization of research on library use suffer the same difficulties as does teaching. This is neither a new problem nor is it restricted to library schools. Research productivity of all types of professional school faculties tends to be lower than it is for the line departments. The teaching demands involved in producing practitioners is in part responsible, but I suspect that the resistance of practicing professionals acts as a brake to university-based research, especially in the newer areas of research on use and users. As evidence for this Table 2 shows the distribution of use studies

TABLE 2

COMPARATIVE ORIGIN OF USE STUDIES

	"LIBRARY SCIENCE DISSERTATIONS"			"BIBLIOGRAPHY OF USE STUDIES"		
	General	Specialized		General	Specialized	
"Inside"	39%	11%	50%	17%	4%	21%
"Outside"	28%	22%	50%	12%	67%	79%
	67%	33%	100%=36	29%	71%	100%=351

among library science Ph.D. dissertations (1925–63)[7] compared to use studies carried on in other settings. These latter are taken from the extensive bibliography on use studies compiled by Richard A. Davis and C. A. Bailey.[8]

From both the annotated list of library-science dissertations and the annotated Davis bibliography, only empirical studies dealing with the use or users of the library were selected. There was no serious difficulty in assigning any of the titles to one of the cells. The results here are illustrative only and should not be misconstrued as defining either the degree of productivity of library schools in general or the quality or content of their research.[9]

From the marginal percentages it is clear that high-level library-school research has been directed toward problems inside rather than outside the library (50 per cent of the empirical dissertations on use), and far more concerned with the general rather than the specialized audience (67 books and libraries). In contrast, the field as a whole, representing researchers far beyond the walls of library schools, shows a considerably different distribution with the emphasis clearly on the specialized audience outside the library—the typical "use" study. If the curriculum and the research direction of the modern library school are to be at least responsive to the problems of its cousins, documentalists and information retrievers, then library-school research priorities should change.

A more compelling reason for a renewed interest in the study of users, however, is the change in the ways knowledge is created and communicated. I can think of no more dramatic way of underlining the rapidity and depth of these changes than to quote the following excerpt from the autobiography of Leonard Woolf who was writing about his experiences at the time of World War I. In less than one lifetime these words seem ironically outdated.

I have often irritated people by saying that an intelligent person can become what is called an "authority" on most "questions," "problems," or "subjects," by intensive study for two or three months. They thought me arrogant for saying so, or if not arrogant, not serious. But it is true. The number and volume of relevant facts on any subject are not many or great and the number of good and important books on it are few. If you have a nose for relevant facts and the trails which lead to them—this is essential and half the battle—and if you know how to work with the laborious pertinacity of a mole and a beaver, you can acquire in a few months all the knowledge necessary for a thorough understanding of the subject.[10]

[7] *Library Science Dissertations: 1925–60—an Annotated Bibliography of Doctoral Studies* (Washington, D.C.: Bureau of Educational Research and Development, Library Services Branch, U.S. Office of Education, 1963). Information about library science dissertations for 1960–63 was obtained from *Library Literature, Dissertation Abstracts,* and the *Library Quarterly.*

[8] *Bibliography of Use Studies* (Philadelphia: Graduate School of Library Science, Drexel Institute of Technology, 1964).

[9] Since they represent a more serious research commitment, Ph.D. dissertations rather than M.A. theses were selected. The Davis bibliography occasionally reports studies in several forms—different research reports, multiple publication, and so forth. Insofar as possible these have been removed, but even with further excision the results do not change appreciably.

[10] Leonard Woolf, *Beginning Again* (London: Hogarth Press, 1964), p. 185.

THE ROLE OF THE PUBLIC LIBRARY: IMPLICATIONS FOR LIBRARY EDUCATION

LEON CARNOVSKY

ABOUT twenty years ago, in an article entitled "Preparation for the Librarian's Profession,"[1] I undertook to identify the characteristics of successful library performance, and against them to project a general program or curriculum which would lead to their acquisition. I do not know how widely the article was read or how seriously it was taken. Upon rereading it, I should characterize it as more a rationale of an existing situation than a prescription for much in the way of change, and therefore it offered no particular reason for attracting much attention. And yet, it seems to me that it said a few things that were not mere reflections of contemporary library education, and that even today, though they still seem valid to me, are not taken too seriously. Indeed, as I shall indicate, there is a current trend which does even greater violence to these points than did the library school of twenty years ago. Since we are here concerned with "intellectual foundations," it is not amiss to suggest that this trend may be in the direction of anti-intellectualism in library education. But more on this later.

To lay the basis for a consideration of library education, let us begin with an indispensable, if obvious, assumption. This is that we cannot begin to plan a curriculum without some conception of purpose. The simpler the purpose the less complex the curriculum; in truth, a very simple purpose may be achieved without a training program at all. If a public library were set up simply to permit access to books, there need be no sophisticated training program involved, and in fact such a program would seem highly pretentious. I suspect that hundreds of small libraries, set up to do no more than this, do it quite satisfactorily with a minimum of administrative supervision. All the talk in the last twenty-five or thirty years advocating the incorporation of such libraries into a larger network (the library system) makes sense only against a vision of changing —perhaps enlarging—their purpose, but basically I should say that simple ends require simple means, and among such means I should not include formal library education.

But the entire history of the public library movement suggests that its progenitors, and, by extension, society at large, saw the library as something much more than this. No one can read the history of the American library without realizing that libraries were advocated because of their potential contribution to the educational, cultural, and moral welfare of the people. Even George Ticknor, with his endlessly quoted reference to the library's providing "the pleasant literature of the day," justified this not as an end in itself but as contributing to an interest in, and demand for, books in "the graver departments of knowledge." Certainly Everett, Wayland, Bates, and others among the forerunners and founders of the Boston Public Library

---

[1] "Preparation for the Librarian's Profession," *Library Quarterly,* XII (July, 1942), 404–11.

were strongly motivated toward the broadly educational impact of the library; and later Andrew Carnegie drew upon his own experience to champion libraries as an educational enterprise. I do not mean to imply that reading for pleasure, for its own sake, was necessarily frowned upon, or that libraries should turn away from it, but this purpose was made secondary to the educational, cultural, and instrumental purpose: to contribute to man's growth intellectually and to help him in his vocation. That this purpose is still very much in our minds is made plentifully evident in the testimony presented to congressional committees to justify increased expenditures for library purposes.

Though one may question whether or not, or the extent to which, this enlarged purpose is necessarily reflected in all libraries, even in libraries of some size, I think it is, depending on the particular library and on its community. Librarians do not buy books solely and exclusively in response to demand for reading representing the least common denominator of literary quality; on the other hand, except in such libraries as the New York Public Library, they rarely respond to the potential esoteric demand for the specialized book, manuscript, or document that an advanced scholar might find useful. Somewhere in the broad spectrum between these two extremes one may place virtually all but the smallest of our public libraries. They *do* have good books, books of literary quality, books of interest and value to the undifferentiated, if limited, audience that might be drawn to them. (Parenthetically, it is always a minority; most people above the age of seventeen or eighteen are not interested in such books or in books of any kind, or do not depend on the public library for them, and do not even register for the privilege of using them.) Most of the people who do want and read good books make their own selection; in bringing about the union of book and reader the library's role is essentially a passive one. It does make its active contribution in the *selection* of these books and in so *arranging* them that the reader can get at them himself and with a minimum of fuss. In saying this I am pinpointing two essential library functions: book selection and book arrangement. The way these functions are performed is bound to vary from library to library. Now the question: Can these functions be taught, are they necessarily the job of the library school, and are they "intellectual"?

First, I should say that whether or not they can be taught, they certainly must be learned. How, or where, it is difficult to say, and I doubt if anyone has the definitive answer. Insofar as book selection is related to a sense of quality in books, the basis must lie in the educational background of the individual charged with the responsibility of selection. Our faith in higher education may be somewhat naïve, but it is all we have; at any rate, it is the faith that library schools—and libraries—have made the basis for admission to the profession and subsequent employment. A long period of contact with books, a subtle cultivation of literary standards and values, a vague apprehension of better and worse—all these we assume, and I think with some justice, are distinguishing characteristics of the bookman. It is easy to impugn higher education and to downgrade the sophistication of college graduates, but we frankly have little more to go on. What this adds up to is, first, that a bookish sense to be applied in book selection is imperative; second, that it is *best* achieved, though not solely, through college education; and third, if it is not achieved there the library school cannot make up for it.

Is the act of selection an intellectual one? If it is based on the bookish sense that I have been talking about, I do not see how it can be denied. It is not something that a machine of whatever sophistication can accomplish, nor is it something that can readily be turned over to one of limited education. But let us be perfectly clear on this matter: if book selection is nothing more than reacting to pressures, whether by individuals, groups, best-seller lists, the decisions of others, it needs no sense of bookishness at all, only an awareness of such pressures and the agility to respond to them. If this is book selection, I should find it difficult to equate it with intellectual foundations. For this reason I doubt the necessity or the efficacy of too much emphasis on an acquaintance with the book-selection aids. Of course, librarians should know about them, and I suspect that they cannot help but learn about them quickly and practically as part of the job. To suggest an analogy, a lawyer must learn his sources for looking up cases, court decisions, and the like, but this knowledge has little to do with his functions as a lawyer.

Under arrangement of books, I have in mind the whole panoply of activities subsumed under the cataloging, classifying, and shelving of books. Here again I should say that if these activities consist only of mechanically following a set of rules, it is difficult to justify them as intellectual. But there are, I believe, at least two respects in which a truly intellectual aspect is involved: one, the construction of the cataloging codes; and the other, the judgment as to when codes and rules are to be disregarded. These are not arbitrary decisions but rather based on mature judgment which, ideally at least, covers such considerations as interrelation of knowledge, semantics, and reader expectations. Knowledge of existing codes is important and must be gained somewhere if not in the library school, but I should regard such knowledge alone as insufficient to the recognition of cataloging and classification as truly intellectual disciplines.

In addition to book selection and arrangement, library service involves the reader relations that we commonly refer to as reference work and reader guidance. How does one prepare for these functions? In reference work I doubt if any library school can go far beyond bare introductions: to acquaint students with major aids in answering questions, to provide some opportunity through practice to learn their virtues and limitations, and to acquire some technical skill in their use. When we consider the mass of reference aids, getting to know them is no small matter; the disheartening thing is that for a good deal of reference work, and the most difficult, a knowledge, however extensive, of the basic tools may be pitifully inadequate. I am sure that for the mass of reference questions raised in public libraries, the encyclopedias, dictionaries, yearbooks, indexes, concordances, books of quotations, *et al.*, are all that are necessary. It is the relatively rare questions—but by no means insignificant in variety and importance —that try the sophistication, imagination, and all-round ability of the reference librarian; and here both experience and broad subject knowledge background seem indispensable. If any preparation beforehand can be given, I believe it should take the form of assignments that go beyond dependence on the conventional reference aids. Let me emphasize that this is preparation or introduction; only wide and continuing experience can create the reference librarian of real stature.

I have considered the functions of book selection and reference work or reader guidance largely from the standpoint of the books themselves, but unless the audience is considered in the process, these functions would proceed in a vacuum. Whatever the value and importance of its contents, a library without readers may have its uses, but it is not a library in the sense commonly accepted. This observation, particularly relevant to the public library, immediately raises the question about knowledge of the reader and about the information and cultural context in which he lives. We need only realize the impact of paperbacks on patterns of reading in the last twenty years to justify raising the question of its implications for library policy. If such matters are not central in library administration, they are at least sufficiently close to warrant serious consideration. But the union of book and reader is an intensely personal matter. Can preparation of librarians include more attention to psychological implications, in the interest of more precisely recommending a reading program to the person in need of and wishing such assistance? This is a long way from the distasteful prescribing or dictating the reading anyone should do; and, indeed, the fear of such an interpretation may have inhibited our attention to it. If reader guidance is to mean anything more than the glib handing out of ready-made reading lists—hardly an intellectual pursuit—we ought to see whether something deeper is involved in adapting books to readers. That this is not done now is no reason why it should not be carefully considered, since we are concerned with the library of the future—its contribution to society and to the individuals who comprise it.

This somewhat pedagogical role is one that librarians would prefer to steer clear of as perhaps inappropriate, yet it is no more inappropriate than the ventures into music, films, and similar areas that librarians have warmly embraced. If it is to become a library function, place will have to be made for it in the preparation of librarians.

Although my comments thus far have been keyed to adult needs and services, they apply even more obviously to children. Book selection for children implies a sense of literary values and the distinction between the better and poorer; and unless the children's librarian is content to base selection solely on the opinion of others as expressed in recommended lists, the ability to make distinctions must be acquired. And if the children's librarian is to be an effective guide to children's reading, obviously some background in child psychology is indispensable. A knowledge of children's literature and a knowledge of children that transcends the affectionate and the sentimental attachment should enter into the makeup of any children's librarian. Whether or not such knowledge is gained in a library school is a secondary consideration; if, as I believe, it is essential, it must be provided somewhere. On the other hand, if it is not essential, the question may well be raised as to any truly intellectual foundations of library work with children.

In any public library a vast number of processes contribute to its smooth operation. These range from the purely mechanical, like book-charging and record-keeping, to what we regard as professional, like reference and bibliographical work. Increasingly we see human activities displaced by mechanical apparatus, and activities once considered professional performed by clerical or non-professional persons. Simple cataloging and ordering of L. C. and Wilson cards cannot qualify as professional tasks; nor can book acquisition based on listing in the *Booklist* or *Standard Catalog* be regarded as a task involving a high degree of intellectual application. This is not to deprecate their importance but simply to indicate that, once relieved of the necessity for looking after such matters, the true professional is in a position to do those things that are not readily intrusted to machines or clerks. I need not repeat the evidence for this trend in industry and in other professions; as Don Swanson reminded us a year ago, "Those operations within libraries which can be reduced to 'clerical' or 'formal' routines are susceptible of mechanization, while those which require professional training and hence the exercise of human judgment or intellect cannot be mechanized."[2] Our job is to develop a curriculum and a program which will enable our students to be truly professional, at the same time making them aware of the whole spectrum of library activity so that they can themselves distinguish between the mechanical and professional.

Turning aside from the internal aspects of individual library operations, let me consider education for librarianship in a somewhat broader framework, and librarianship itself as a broad social movement. In short, I shall try to identify certain areas that every librarian should be familiar with, even though they may not directly affect his competence as a functioning librarian.

I begin with library history. History is often justified for its instrumental values—to keep us from repeating past mistakes, to learn by experience. There undoubtedly is something to this, but I believe that history needs no instrumental justification to merit a place in a library-school curriculum. But the history I have in mind is not the memorization of dates and events but rather the history of the library seen in its contemporary setting. I mean by this the social forces that contributed to the emergence of the library and that brought about a change in its character and form. Thus I am less interested in the claims for Gutenberg or Coster as the inventor of printing from movable type than I am in the impact that the invention has had on the transmission and dissemination of ideas and how it led to the evolution and development of the library as we know it today. I frankly doubt if knowledge of this kind is altogether necessary for the making of a librarian, any more than a knowledge of medical history is necessary to the surgeon; still, I think it can be justified for its own sake, and conceivably such historical perspective may help the librarian in more clearly visualizing and formulating his own appropriate goals.

A second area embraces an appreciation of the elements in contemporary civilization that may serve to promote

---

[2] "Dialogues with a Catalog," *Library Quarterly*, XXXIV (January, 1964), 125.

dependence on the library on the one hand, and to de-emphasize it on the other. Surely it is not too much to expect librarians to know and to comprehend such relevant social trends as the growth and movement of populations, the rise of urbanism and metropolitanism, the increase in numbers attending school, the rapid proliferation of institutions of higher education, etc. All these trends have their impact upon the extent and character of public library use; the potential librarian should become aware of them. He should also have some awareness of the immense change taking place in the general pattern of communication of ideas and information. I have already mentioned the impact of the paperback, and there is some evidence of its influence on library circulation; we also have some evidence of the interplay of television and reading. We know, for example, that television may stimulate as well as substitute for reading, though such knowledge remains highly limited and crudely generalized. How much closer to exact knowledge we can come is a moot question, but I do not see how we can logically determine the library's functions without devoting some attention to other media, print and non-print, that satisfy informational and recreational needs. The library's program may be shaped in part not only by what has historically been expected of it but also by what it currently needs to do because no other agency can do it so well.

Related to the influence that social forces have upon library goals is their achievement. How large must a library be to reach the goals it may have set? Such a query leads the librarian into the realm of library government and organization, and the possibility, perhaps the necessity, of changing traditional forms of library structure. Such consideration involves some knowledge of library standards, how they have been arrived at, their logic and their acceptability, as well as their application to libraries with purposes other, or more limited, than those on which the standards presumably have been based. The relationship of library organization to finance and to performance—in short, what difference does it make?—is a matter that librarians must reckon with; they must enter the profession unwilling to accept prescribed dogma and with the urge to raise questions and to challenge in a sense of honest inquiry. Although in a society as mercurial as ours there can never be final answers, the very process of raising relevant questions is an intellectual one.

Because a potential librarian must begin to comprehend how and in what ways a library is made to tick, the library school provides courses in administration. The scope of such courses is wide and includes just about everything not accounted for in courses on book selection and bibliography, cataloging and classification, and reference work. The three major divisions in courses in administration are government, finance, and personnel, with such matters as co-operative and contractual agreements, public relations, codes of ethics, etc., frequently introduced as well. How much of what is included is essential or desirable is debatable. Much, frankly, may be highly unrealistic, measured against practical applications. Even if the library-school graduate were immediately to step into a responsible administrative position—and few graduates do—he would have to adapt himself to existing laws, ordinances, regulations, etc., for which no course of preparation can be adequate and, indeed, is frequently irrelevant. If this is the case for the few who at once become library administrators, how much truer for those whose rise to administration is still several years ahead —by which time they will have forgotten what they were taught, or the conditions will have so changed as to bear little relation to what they once learned. This is not to denigrate the teaching of administration in library schools but to suggest an emphasis on principles broad enough to provide a sound theoretical base whatever the local situation or the current way of doing things. There *are* principles of public finance, there *is* a theory of personnel administration derived from the field of public administration, and these are the matters we should teach, rather than the pat (often unrealistic) solutions to problems a student may never encounter. The same thing is true in the area of government; an administrator quickly discovers what the members of his library board are like and the laws that determine the status of his library. But he ought to know the library's backgrounds as a local or state responsibility, the place of boards in public administration, and why library boards persist when the board form has been discarded in so many other areas of state and municipal authority. None of the foregoing is intended to imply that budget-making, recruitment, campaigns for more money, public relations, or codes of ethics are unimportant; they obviously are important, but I should hope that the major concern in any administration course would be that of broad, pervasive principles rather than how-to-do-it formulas. Only to the extent that such principles are stressed can the foundations of any course in administration be intellectual in any real sense.

Having made the point that we should be training for the long run and not only for immediacy, let me introduce another area of concern to the future librarian: systems planning. Since this topic will be treated extensively in other papers, I shall limit my observations to a few sentences. We are all aware of the impact automation is making in all our lives, and the library is certainly not immune. One need only mention the MEDLARS operation at the National Library of Medicine and the potential automation in the Library of Congress to remind us that here are real, not fanciful, developments. The contributions and limitations of automation must be recognized, and the librarian who is completely innocent of its library applications will be bypassed by others more sophisticated in such matters. Therefore the library school must provide a basic knowledge in the relevance of the computer to library operations—under what conditions automation would be economical, under what conditions it would not.

I have already discussed intellectual aspects of book selection, but now I should add the desirability of attention to the general area of free speech, the freedom to read, and its control, or censorship. The literature, both philosophical and legal, is vast, in keeping with the significance of the topic. Basically, the decision whether to buy or not to buy is a moral one—what is *right,* rather than what is expedient or safe—and every librarian should have some intellectual grasp of the fundamental problems involved. One need only read a few of the decisions of judges in censorship cases to realize the complexity of the problem. To what extent, for example, should the views of literary critics prevail in judging whether or not a novel is within the safeguards of the first amendment? What do we mean by community standards? Can a jury of twelve be equated with community standards in deciding what is obscene? What does the phrase "redeeming social importance" mean? How, if at all, can this be determined? Is free speech an absolute, and if not, what are its appropriate limitations—and do these boundaries change as society itself changes? Answers to these questions are anything but easy, yet they are all important, and they deserve serious attention in any library training program.

In summary, and with the public library primarily but not exclusively in mind, I shall list the major areas of knowledge or competence for the potential librarian.

1. *Book selection.*—I use this term to cover the vague concept of bookishness, the ability to distinguish qualitatively among books and including some literary grasp. Knowledge of trade, subject, and national bibliography, of book sources, of the second-hand book trade, of book reviewing media, is important; but basically I believe the librarian must be a bookman.

2. *Arrangement and organization of the collection.*—Classification and cataloging are the indispensable elements here; once more, though classification systems like Dewey and L.C. should be mastered, as well as cataloging rules and codes, I should expect serious attention to be devoted to principles in the organization of knowledge and to the logic which underlies the construction of cataloging codes. Whatever the practical applications, if any, at least an introduction to comparative codes would be welcome.

3. *Guidance to readers.*—This phrase embraces reference work and reader assistance and goes considerably beyond an acquaintance with the conventional, most frequently consulted, reference tools. It involves, too, some knowledge of psychology, as a basis for professional aid to the reader of limited background or reading ability.

4. *Administration.*—Here I have in mind primarily an acquaintance with broad principles of government, finance, and personnel.

5. *Library history and setting.*—An understanding of library backgrounds and of the social forces which led to the library and which subsequently shaped its character, together with an awareness of contemporary trends—in population, education, communication media, and the like.

6. *Systems planning.*—The identification of library requirements in light of library functions, including an awareness of the potential contribution of automation; in short, a consideration of future library design and structure.

7. *The freedom to read.*—Its philosophical and legal backgrounds.

These areas contribute to the intellectual foundations of librarianship. They are not presented as discrete courses or even presented as a curriculum, for many of the abilities implied or prescribed in this outline cannot be taught in a course or even in a single year. Some abilities require a broad educational background, altogether divorced from library training as such; for others, courses must be provided outside the library school itself. Within the library school, the scheme of course organization will dictate what is to be included in given courses, what new courses are desirable. My emphasis falls on what I conceive to be the ideal librarian, the librarian as a professional with a firm intellectual underpinning, not on the structure of a series of courses.

This conception of the ideal public librarian is not necessarily at variance from that held by some, if not all, of the present library schools. Book selection, reference services, and the organization of books are taught in all of them; other areas are likely to be represented though they may be considered as of peripheral interest only. It is not only a question, however, of whether or not the seven areas suggested are reflected in the existing curriculums, but *how* they are presented that determines the intellectual challenge involved. As I stated elsewhere:

> The best any library school can do is to turn out persons capable of *becoming* librarians—librarians of vision and imagination, persons able to adapt their theoretical backgrounds to a practical situation. No two libraries are alike; public libraries differ from school libraries, and even one public library differs sharply from another. Given a solid background of theory and principle, a well-trained person should not have difficulty in adapting himself to the practices of all but the most specialized kind of library. . . . The real distinction is between the apprenticeship to a craft and preparation for a profession. Both have their place, and neither is lacking in dignity and importance. The line between them is not sharp, nor need it be; many of the so-called theoretical elements will surely form part of the apprentice training, and many of the skills will have to be mastered as part of professional study. Indeed, it is difficult to conceive of the professional librarian devoid of a thorough mastery of the technical aspects of his calling . . . it is incumbent upon all library school administrators and faculties to engage in continual self-examination, in an effort to eliminate the nonessential, the trivial, the routines and details that are readily learned on the job. Let them bear in mind that no matter how thoroughly they try to prepare for all aspects of all types of libraries, they cannot altogether succeed, for each library has elements of uniqueness that can be learned there and nowhere else.[3]

But there are matters that cannot be learned in a library or even in a library school; these are the qualities that broadly if vaguely contribute to the making of an educated person. For this reason the library profession generally has insisted upon college education as preliminary to professional preparation. We all realize, of course, that the nature of such education is more important than the four years allocated to it, or to the fact that they culminate in a degree. But compromises and decisions have to be made, and without attempting to spell out what a general education consists of, the Standards for Accreditation of Library Schools specify three basic requirements for admission: "(*a*) graduation from an approved college or university, (*b*) adequacy of background in general and special subject education, and (*c*) scholarship to meet the standards for graduate study in the institution." These requirements may imply that satisfactory mastery of library techniques depends on four years of college—a dubious implication, certainly, for some techniques which may be readily learned by persons lacking college preparation—or, more likely, they reflect the conviction that whatever else it takes to be a librarian, a solid education is essential. This is not the place to review the almost infi-

[3] "Education for Librarianship," PNLA, *Library Development Project Reports*, Vol. IV: *Libraries and Librarians of the Pacific Northwest* (Seattle: University of Washington Press, 1960), pp. 207–8.

nite variations from college to college, from student to student, from one curriculum to another, or the varying conceptions of the vague phrase "liberal education." But that these variations exist is no reason to throw up our hands and deny the importance of college education, and therefore I should deplore any attempt to eliminate or compromise with this requirement.

I emphasize what may seem an obvious point because there are stirrings within the profession which move in a direction contrary to the one suggested as leading to the creation of the ideal librarian, and which, if realized, would prove disastrous to professional librarianship. I refer to the current agitation to make library training part of the four-year college program. I do not deny for a moment that a college junior or senior has the ability to learn library techniques and even to become an acceptable practitioner; I do question whether the compromise implied in this reduction of the period of general education is wise. I should be less averse to this if the library-science courses at the undergraduate level had real intellectual content, but I strongly suspect that they consist of precisely the kind of vocational how-to-do-it instruction that should be de-emphasized in the graduate program.

The pressure for undergraduate library instruction has come from sorely harrassed librarians faced with critical personnel shortages; given the choice of employing four-year college graduates without library training (and thus forced to some form of in-service training) and college graduates part of whose program includes such training, they urge more of the latter. Thus a recent recommendation comes from the New York Library Association to the director of that state's Division of Library Extension that requirements for assignment to the civil service classification of junior librarian be changed to permit assigning the grade to "graduates of approved four-year college programs, including one full year of training in Library Science, who have passed the certification examination."[4] This is illustrative of pressures that are evident in many other parts of the country. The net result must inevitably be to water down the general education program and to relax emphasis upon liberal education.

One may sympathize with the plight of the employer without agreeing that the proposed solution is desirable or necessary. In any event, we should recognize that librarianship needs persons of more, not less, general education, and cutting down the period of general education is a step backward. In all fairness it should be noted that undergraduate library training does not always displace liberal education but takes the place of other vocational training. (The catalogs of teacher-training institutions, now called universities, provide depressing evidence of the prevalence of vocationalism in their four-year programs.) If it were only a question of substituting one vocation for another, I should find little to object to. What I should much prefer is the elimination of *all* such vocational programs at the undergraduate level; what I should like to see is a potential

---

[4] The recommendation continues: "Such persons would be granted a provisional public librarian's certificate, indefinitely renewable. In order to obtain a permanent certificate, however, any candidate from this group must acquire one additional full year's education at an approved college or university, or its equivalent" ("Recommendations of Certification Committee to Director, Division of Library Extension," February 6, 1964 [mimeographed]).

librarian with the kind of educational background that would enhance his intellectual stature.

Henry Thoreau's observation on reading may be cited to bring this paper to a close:

> Most men have learned to read to serve a paltry convenience, as they have learned to cipher in order to keep accounts and not be cheated in trade; but of reading as a noble intellectual exercise they know little or nothing; yet this only is reading, in a high sense, not that which lulls us as a luxury and suffers the nobler faculties to sleep the while, but what we have to stand on tiptoe to read and devote our most alert and wakeful hours to.[5]

Reading as a noble intellectual exercise is not all of librarianship, but public librarianship without this vision is something of a betrayal of the high hopes held for it, both historically and contemporaneously. In presenting the suggestions for a program of education for public librarians, I have been motivated in part by a desire to see us produce librarians with the vision of reading—and, by extension, of librarianship—as seen by Thoreau.

[5] *Walden; or Life in the Woods* (New York: E. P. Dutton & Co., 1908), pp. 91–92.

THE SYSTEMS APPROACH TO LIBRARY PLANNING

MERRILL M. FLOOD

WE ARE all concerned with the intellectual foundations of library education, each with a view from his own vantage point. Those of you whose professional lives are devoted to the library field must view our common problem by extrapolation from your own past experiences, guided also by your insights and hopes, but with an awareness of exciting prospects for new advances as technological progress on all fronts yields its harvest of better tools and improved understanding. Those of us whose primary work lies outside the library field view these prospects with great expectations and enthusiasm, for our need as users of information is an urgent one during this period that has been so aptly described as one of "information explosion."

My own special vantage point is that of an outsider to the library field, an insider in scientific research, and thus an avid consumer of information, an insider in the education of systems engineers and applied mathematicians, and an insider in the application of the systems approach. Now the systems approach to a planning, design, or operations problem, in whatever area of application, is itself an ill defined but powerful concept. Briefly and simply, the systems approach to any problem requires that no artificial bounds be placed on matters that can be considered in the search for a solution to the problem.

The field of system engineering, as pioneered by the Bell Telephone Laboratories, is described well by the following statement:

The Systems Engineer studies advances in basic science and technology and translates them into new means for meeting the expanding requirements of the System. After establishing both technical and economic feasibility, he conceives, plans and recommends to management new systems which will ultimately be developed and designed in detail by others. He monitors and supports this development and evaluates performance through field trials and measurements of working systems.

If the word "library" is inserted before the word "systems" each time it occurs in this statement, we have a workable definition of the library systems engineer. If, instead, we insert the word "communications," then we have essentially the job description for a systems engineer published by the Bell Telephone Laboratories in an employment advertisement in the *New York Times* of August 17, 1958.

It seems evident to me that the systems approach to library planning, to be practiced eventually by trained library systems engineers, should be one major goal of library education of the future. Therefore we shall explore the likely nature of the intellectual content of that part of future curriculums designed to provide the kind of education and training needed by those library school graduates of the future who are expected to take the systems approach to library-planning problems.

If we are to identify the intellectual content of curricular subjects that are apt to be useful in the future to those concerned with the systems approach to library planning, it will be necessary to have some working concept of the library of the future. Indeed, the actual course of library education should in turn exert great influence upon the course of development of the library system. Thus any concept that is widely accepted now to guide library system development will itself affect this development, whether or not the concept adopted is indeed a superior one among all those available. The particular library system concept implied throughout this paper should be considered simply as one of the many worthy of consideration and is used now entirely as a guide to curriculum discussion. However, it would seem highly desirable to follow this same procedure in making actual decisions regarding educational programs, even though quite different concepts may be selected as the ones actually to guide library system development.

All of the libraries, and other information collections, constitute the total library system. This totality throughout the world can be divided geographically by countries, by states, by companies, and in many other ways. The library may be rather easily identified as the content of a single building in a small educational institution, for example, but it will be scattered through many buildings in one of our major universities, or throughout an entire state, as in the University of California. It is not possible to separate the entire library system into subordinate parts, even relatively independent of each other, because of the tremendous interaction between parts—and to the advantage of all. This interdependence leads inevitably to major attempts to standardize methods and procedures for library operation, as reflected in the activities of the entire library profession.

It will be helpful to make some distinction between the total information system and the total library system, for present purposes, even though this distinction cannot be precise and sharp. A great deal of information is exchanged in temporary or semipermanent form, as in ordinary conversations or by radio transmission or by circulation of magazines and newspapers. If the information is recorded in some lasting form, as by printing or a magnetic-tape recording, then this "record" often becomes a part of an organized "collection." These collections become part of the library system when they are organized for some kind of systematic access to the records within them, in contrast to a pile of records to be burned or an archive planned for quite infrequent access.

It is the organization of a collection of records, rather than its mere existence as a collection, that makes it a part of the library system. By the same token a newspaper, magazine, menu, photograph, painting, or any other record becomes a part of the library system only after it is organized as a part of a collection to which access has been provided in some systematic manner. In a sentence, a library is a collection of records together with a retrieval procedure.

The total library system includes the libraries and the persons responsible for them, along with the concepts and procedures that guide the planning and operation of the entire system. In these terms, the systems approach to library planning must take into account the selection and preservation of records appropriate for each collection, the development of retrieval procedures adequate to give the users effective access to the collections, the selection and development of personnel responsible for all phases of library system operation, and the physical plant and other resources forming the system. Above all else, the systems approach must start from a workable concept defining the fundamental purpose of the library system. Most difficult of all, the concept must be stated clearly enough to make it possible to choose between alternative system proposals presented for consideration.

There are library-planning problems at many different levels of complexity. We cannot discuss each separately, great as are the differences, for our purpose is to draw some valid generalizations regarding the intellectual content of a library curriculum intended to serve and be useful at all levels. We have one example of such differences when we compare the problem of planning a national library system for a highly developed country, already well endowed with libraries, with that of a small, newly developed nation having almost no library facilities at all. Or, when planning the development of a public library for a small town, as contrasted with that for a large city, or for a small industrial firm in contrast to that for a giant corporation, we see a few instances of the great disparity in complexity of problems to be solved. From another and more realistic standpoint, we can also see that these problems all have a great deal in common, and it is with this view that we suggest certain basic ingredients of the systems approach as ones useful to library planners at all levels.

The library system of the United States has developed in parallel with our educational system; in both cases the major proportion of the system has been governmentally supported and operated. In addition, both systems have been the fortunate recipients of generous gifts and endowments from private organizations and individuals. We have come to think of education and libraries as something free and available to all citizens, to a high degree, as one of the rights and advantages of living in this great nation. As with our transportation system, our postal system, and many other services, partial or total subsidization has accustomed us to the acceptance of educational and library benefits as free, even though we realize that we support them indirectly through taxation. On the other hand, a regulated utility like the telephone system gives us similar services for which we pay more or less directly, and we have also come to accept this as a desirable and natural method of operation. The postal system, like the telephone system, is operated essentially on a centralized national basis, even though one system is governmental and the other is privately operated. In none of these cases do we have the capability of assessing the real social and economic value of the systems but must rely instead upon changing demands as a sufficient cause for modification of each system. So it is with the library system at all levels, for we are unable to assess the returns from an increase in library service in terms of the social and economic benefits to the users. This fact makes the application of the systems approach difficult because of the lack of an acceptable measure for assessing the advantage of one proposed library alternative over the other, but we have suffered through this difficulty in many other areas, especially in the general area of national defense.

The library profession as a whole has a great opportunity to raise its aspiration level an order of magnitude during the coming decade. There is a broad and growing general public awareness of an urgent need for a greatly improved system for bringing recorded information more quickly and more surely to many segments of the general population. This need is felt with particular urgency by the many workers in science and technology, where the rate of production of new knowledge during the past decade has been so great that in many fields older information is nearly valueless. The library profession is working heroically and in a dedicated manner to keep up with this need, but there seems to be a growing awareness that something more is needed than further extensions and improvements of traditional library tools and techniques. On the other hand, we have all learned that major advances do not result simply from adaptation of some new technological resource, such as the modern electronic computer, for the entire library profession and the potential users must all work in concert for a considerable period of evolution in adjusting to the use of even the most promising new tool or technique. This evolutionary process can be accelerated to a considerable degree by application of the systems approach if adopted by a substantial number of members of the library profession working in harmony with others from other disciplines who can be enlisted to join in the effort. Looking ahead, by all odds the best hope for significant progress toward this end is through the educational process, and it is toward this end that we make our present proposals for emphasis in the library curriculums of the future on subjects and disciplines supporting the systems approach.

These very general comments hardly provide the basis for a productive start on a library-planning problem by a competent systems engineer, even if he were also fully versed in all aspects of librarianship. He would need to translate these philosophical remarks into working assumptions adequate at least to guide his preliminary thinking, and these broad assumptions would eventually have to be translated again into quite precise engineering terms before he could use them as the basis for a specification of his library system design. I recently had occasion to start this process as a member of the survey team under the chairmanship of Gilbert W. King that was concerned with the broad problem of automating a large research library such as the Library of Congress; and I shall list a few of these assumptions to illustrate their general nature. These are my personal assumptions, and they are not entirely consistent with the recommendations made by the survey team in the published report, *Automation and the Library of Congress*.[1] However, those who are familiar with this report may safely assume that it proposed a national library system much like the one assumed here.

For present purposes, we shall take as our problem a consideration of the steps that should be taken during the coming decade to modernize the entire research library operation in the United States. This may appear to be a grandiose task; but it could be quite misleading to give serious consideration to the problem of modernizing one research library, not taken as simply a part of a national effort, because of the great economies that will surely be realized through standardization and systematic interchanges between re-

[1] Gilbert W. King *et al.*, *Automation and the Library of Congress* (Washington, D.C.: Library of Congress, 1963).

search libraries. In any event, the planner of any particular library must surely take into account his expectations with respect to the development of the national library system during the coming decade.

The grand strategy I favor, in approaching any major system-engineering task, is to start with the highest goals imaginable—to be achieved at a ridiculously optimistic rate—and resist, but sometimes succumb to, realities that force lesser goals and slower achievement upon us. I have presented this point of view, with examples from my personal experience, in a recent paper.[2]

Our sample of assumptions will be divided into three groups: *first*, social assumptions, relating to needs and benefits; *second*, political assumptions, relating to support possibilities and organization; and *third*, technological assumptions, which relate to components and feasibility. The assumptions all relate to the problem of planning a "modernized library system," hereafter referred to as MLS.

SOCIAL ASSUMPTIONS

Information that is useful for the purposes of large research libraries is not all stored now in those libraries. For example, in the field of scientific research, technical reports and memoranda often are never brought into the library system or are brought in too late to be of maximum value.

Assumption S1 (completeness). *All information, in whatever form, that is potentially useful for any type of study, research, or inquiry, will be considered for inclusion in the MLS.*

---

[2] Merrill M. Flood, "System Engineering," *Management Technology*, I (1960), 21–35.

Information services that are economically desirable and technologically feasible, but not yet available, will be included in the MLS. This includes such obvious gains as those possible through the substitution of lower-cost personnel (or equipment) for system users, when time saved or other savings to the users exceed added system cost; current examples include user waiting, or user travel to the system, and the like. This also includes less obvious gains, such as values to the user through faster delivery of information, or through presentation of information in better form.

Assumption S2 (efficiency). *The choice between any two alternative proposed designs for the MLS will be made on the basis of an appraisal of all costs and gains, direct and indirect, and without regard to the sources of immediate support.*

A central difficulty in providing a complete and efficient MLS stems from the fact that there will not always be an even balance between the ability of the individual user to pay for information and the actual cost of providing it. There are innumerable examples of this social imbalance; one is the student and another is the patient. The student typifies the social asset under development, and the invalid typifies the normally able participant who is disabled by chance.

Certain inefficient services would not be provided, even though some class of user might be very willing and able to pay for them. As an extreme example, military and economic information of value to a potential enemy nation would not be available to all who could pay.

Assumption S3 (financing). *Each class of user of the MLS will be charged according to his ability to pay, as meas-*

ured by the maximum amount he would pay rather than forego the service, with a uniform policy for charges within a particular class of users.

Whenever any activity is automated, there is a necessary redirection and relocation of some persons previously engaged in the activity. We have learned during the past decade that in this transition to automation we must take careful and systematic account of the social costs and values due to the change, if otherwise desirable design alternatives are not to be discarded improperly because of inadequate attention to transitional needs.

Assumption S4 (transition). *Each class of participant in the present library system will be protected against economic loss or professional displacement due to the transition to an automated MLS.*

POLITICAL ASSUMPTIONS

My political assumptions will be as pessimistic as my social assumptions were optimistic. This is the conservative choice, in both cases, since it probes toward social optimization under the restrictions of political reality. In other words, the objective is to optimize socially under given environmental limitations. Similarly, our technological assumptions will be optimistic as to eventual technical feasibility but pessimistic as to timing of new developments.

The general public, and our responsible governmental agencies, do not yet seem ready to plunge into modernization of our library system as a desirable goal all by itself. They prefer to show some practical needs, as for education, defense, science, space, or competition with the Soviet Union. As with our decision to develop the atomic bomb or to proceed vigorously with our space program, the decision to modernize our national library system will certainly not be based on detailed systems analyses of costs versus benefits. Nor can we predict even the nature of the major benefits that will accrue from a vast increase in the capability of our library system when modernization is finally undertaken, just as we could not predict in advance the nature of the most important products deriving from our support of atomic energy projects or the space venture.

The information explosion is perhaps even more important to control for our benefit than is the space venture. Everyone would agree that the store of knowledge is increasing beyond our ability to utilize it effectively, even for educational and research purposes; there are also huge opportunities for significant improvement in managing other major stores of information, such as legal and industrial files. The capabilities of future information-processing systems are beyond our present range of imagination, and it seems certain that many previously sophisticated human intellectual activities will be supplanted by new types of synthetically intelligent machines. The MLS should eventually make available to people, and to other machines, fragments from the store of knowledge as they are needed for all important purposes.

As one example, we may consider the problem of arranging the store of knowledge, or library, so that physicians and public health specialists can utilize it most effectively. Although I am unable to specify the nature of the new system, I am convinced that some better way can and should be found for storage and retrieval of knowledge relevant to maintenance of health than is presently on the horizon. The National Medical Library, and *Index Medicus* and MEDLARS, constitute a fine example of modern librarianship; but the vigorous movement, spearheaded by the National Institutes of Health, to establish major new medical information-processing centers is sure to lead to some kind of coupling between library sources and practitioners working toward the improvement of health. Thus the MLS must include a medical collection adequate both for the medical specialist and for those primarily interested in non-medical specialties, all arranged for retrieval and processing in new manners and for new types of functions.

We have tried to establish the fact that the political climate is good for making a major move toward an MLS. We have also remarked that the MLS is politically less wanted than is modernization of systems serving special purposes, such as health, education, science, and so forth. This suggests that support, both financial and intellectual, is more readily available for modernizing various special information processing functions than it would be for the MLS as such.

Assumption P1 (need). *The need for modernization of the national system for storage and retrieval of knowledge has been well recognized in certain special areas, such as defense, science, education, space, health, and law; an MLS is politically possible now only if such special needs are first met, but these special subsystems can and should be designed to be systematically integrated into an effective over-all MLS.*

Assumption P2 (sponsor). *The federal government is the only possible sponsor for the development of an MLS of radically different design, because the cost would be many millions of dollars over the coming decade.*

Assumption P3 (responsibility). *A single federal agency would almost surely have operating budget and responsibility for the development of an MLS, but the existing libraries would certainly have to be full working partners in any such development.*

TECHNOLOGICAL ASSUMPTIONS

There is a vast literature in the field of library science and a considerable recent literature in the scientific documentation field. The Russian efforts are ambitious and noteworthy. Periodical reports by the National Science Foundation keep us informed on newer information-handling systems, and relevant research and development; various publications in the computer- and information-sciences fields report recent developments relevant to this aspect of library modernization.

The VINITI effort in Russia shows that a vast program is required for progress with the library problem on the national scale, whether or not recent developments in information-processing equipment are taken into account. Recent attempts to develop automated information retrieval systems, such as for the patent system, have made it clear that a great deal of research will be needed before automated systems can be used effectively to process information within a large collection. Eventually, most of us feel that advances in information-processing technology will yield storage and retrieval systems of great capacity and with rapid access, but for the coming decade it seems that these advances will be modest indeed. Such considerations lead to acceptance of tentative but broad technical hypotheses like the following.

Assumption T1 (searching). *There will be no way to scan the entire collection in response to each query; the collection must be searched selectively.*

Assumption T2 (coding). *There is as yet no theory that shows how to code an item in a collection so as to maximize the likelihood of successful retrieval over expected queries.*

Assumption T3 (description). *Some description of the item will be in the collection, and searching for retrieval will be based on these descriptions; the descriptions will be changed from time to time.*

Among the many methods already devised for purposes of description, coding and searching are subject classification, uniterms, subject indexes, citation indexes, superposition coding, and so forth. Although we have some excellent theoretical work on narrow aspects of the description problem, like that of Mooers and Maloney[3] on superposition coding, we seem not to have even a start on any generally useful theoretical basis as a foundation for a solution of the indexing problem.

There seems to be fairly general agreement that the classical approach to description by means of a universal classification of knowledge, from Aristotle to Ranganathan, is not a way that will work. Even though some of these methods work reasonably well for small collections (thousands of records) it seems generally agreed that some very different scheme will be needed for very large collections (millions of records).

One barrier to easy handling of conventional information is its variety of form. There are not only the differences in physical format and in languages used for prose but also differences such as those between prose and maps, photographs and magnetic tape, or alphanumeric and graphic records. While it is true that most or all of these forms of information can be reduced to a superficially common form, such as through scanning and digitalization, this always leaves the differences of meaning. Promising research on standardizing syntactics or on canonical forms for language indicates that we may someday have usable advances in the standardization of language. Meanwhile, systems designed during the next decade or so will profit but little from such research results.

Assumption T4 (language). *Descriptions will be numeric and, essentially, standardized forms of excerpts from the records in the collection.*

Although there are several really exciting new devices that will surely be useful in future information systems there is no one or several devices that dominate the system design consideration. For example, neither the "best" available computer, nor the "best" available microform, nor the "best" available memory, nor the "best" available printer, is clearly the "best" as part of any particular integrated information system.

Assumption T5 (hardware). *Almost any device that can be conceptualized can be developed, if elapsed time and total cost are not considered, but economically justifiable and timely systems must simply be invented or discovered.*

The essence of the argument here is that a very complex system, such as an

---

[3] Calvin N. Mooers, "Zatacoding and Development in Information Retrieval," *ASLIB Proceedings*, VIII (1956), 3–22; Clifford J. Maloney, "Abstract Theory of Retrieval Coding," *International Conference on Scientific Information, 1958* (Washington, D.C.: National Academy of Sciences—National Research Council, 1959), II, 1365–82.

MLS, must be invented or discovered without more help from general scientific and engineering principles than is normally available for devices or components. Or, to put it differently, we shall be entirely unable to decide whether or not library automation is now possible and desirable without first creating fairly specific proposed systems to compare and evaluate relative to each other and the present system. An alternative approach, which I have here called discovery, is to encourage many groups to try out their own individual hunches and ideas until some one or a few such experiences fit more obviously into a desirable, new integrated system. An extreme instance of an approach to discovery is to give at least one group substantial enough resources, and a broad enough charter, so that it can develop and operate a new large library on a purely experimental basis—or, equivalently, to delegate system-management responsibility to one group able to explore imaginatively.

A few additional technical feelings of my own follow without discussion or defense.

Assumption T6 (shelving). *Library records will be "shelved" without regard to their contents, with minor exceptions, on the basis of economical space and handling requirements. Presumably, most present types of library records could be placed in standard containers of proper size and construction, but without binding and without labeling except for an identifying alphanumeric code (shelf number). The piece and container would be permanently joined by their common shelf number.*

Assumption T7 (microform). *It will be standard practice to reduce each record to microform, whether or not the original record is retained, in such a way that the system can automatically retrieve and copy (or print) from a designated portion of the microform record.*

Assumption T8 (transmission). *Microform records will be available to library users through remote viewers, with suitable controls for "browsing" through the microform records of whatever indexes and descriptors are used in the search and retrieval subsystem.*

Assumption T9 (sequencing). *The console operated by the user in controlling the viewer will enable him to search sequentially through the retrieval steps, and through the transmitted record.*

Assumption T10 (association). *The system will include a machine to assist the user in making associations, as proposed by Vannevar Bush for the Memex, while browsing or searching.*

Assumption T11 (teaching). *The system will "teach" the user during use. As a simple example, if the user tries to instruct the system to list all the records meeting certain descriptive conditions, when there are an unreasonably large number of them, then the system will first advise the user of this fact.*

Assumption T12 (learning). *The system will "learn" from users. As a possible example, retrieval search patterns and strategies will be varied according to characteristics of recent users and the particular user at hand. In fact the system might well receive as input some description of the current user and return this to him in modified form as a result of his use of the system that time.*

Assumption T13. *The system will take the initiative in notifying users of records of possible interest. For example, announcements will be selected, printed, and mailed automatically to users on a special list—a new record could be the subject of interest, or an old record could suddenly be discovered to be of interest to a user due to his other recent uses of the library.*

We may now take this list of topics as a sample of those important for future planning of library systems and reinterpret them in terms of curricular needs for library education. These needs are directly related to the application of the systems approach to library planning and are in addition to the many other educational requirements for future members of the library profession.

Systems-engineering methodology is our starting point. Education and training in this area should include the following four course areas: general conceptual background, specific techniques, use of special tools, and case studies. During the next few years, much of the content for these course areas will have to be borrowed from non-library fields and adapted to library educational purposes.

General conceptual background for systems engineering is provided by a growing number of excellent texts and articles treating this topic. Hall's textbook[4] developed for Bell Telephone Laboratories use, stressing experiences in the communications-engineering field, presents excellent examples of systems-engineering projects and includes discussions of the systems approach along with applications of specific techniques —such as information theoretical analyses. The textbook of Goode and Machol[5] stresses experiences in the weapons-systems area, with particular attention to information-processing systems, and includes brief technical summaries of several special techniques often found to be useful in systems-engineering projects—such as queueing theory, linear programming theory, statistical decision theory, game theory, information theory, and digital computer simulation; this text has been used for several years at the graduate course level in the electrical engineering department of the University of Michigan. Proceedings of systems-engineering conferences, handbooks for systems engineers, and articles in a wide variety of periodicals present new materials at a rapidly expanding rate in forms suitable for use at all levels of the library educational process. We shall certainly soon see the publication of library systems engineering papers and textbooks adequate to meet this particular professional need, and more effectively so as the systems approach to library planning yields direct experience with concepts, techniques, and tools especially useful for library techniques.

Specific techniques, such as linear programming and computer simulation, will certainly prove to be useful in library systems engineering as they have in a wide variety of other systems projects. Techniques for the design of experiments and the analysis of experimental data, including applications of probability theory and uses of computers, will certainly be widely used in library systems-engineering projects just as they have been in every other area utilizing the methodology of science and

---

[4] Arthur David Hall, *A Methodology for Systems Engineering* (Princeton, N.J.: D. Van Nostrand Co., 1962).

[5] Harry H. Goode and Robert Engle Machol, *System Engineering: An Introduction to the Design of Large-Scale Systems* (New York: McGraw-Hill Book Co., 1957).

engineering. It also seems safe to predict that many new techniques will be needed and developed for use in treating library problems, for they deal with linguistic and other non-arithmetic forms of information that seem unlikely to be represented well by mathematical theories or computer simulations in which only arithmetical and logical operations are utilized. However, current work on mathematical theories of language, on simulation of cognitive processes, on artificial intelligence, and in other areas of the emerging "information sciences" holds great promise for the future of techniques useful to the library systems engineer. As a single example, it is an impressive fact that Gilbert W. King and his colleagues have succeeded in producing useful translations from Russian to English with present-day data-processing equipment but no underlying formal theory of linguistics.[6]

Special tools, such as the stored-program digital computer and rapid-access microform files, will inevitably find their place in library systems of the future. An interesting example of an attempt to make use of such new tools as components of a large automated research library is discussed in the report of the King survey team. The systems-engineering approach led to the conclusion that current information system technology makes it possible to have a retrieval procedure for identifying records in a large collection in which the user queries the collection directly and sequentially at a console providing nearly instantaneous response to his questions. Since these consoles can be operated at any distance from the central processor, and over the regular communication net, this kind of system could make the entire collection accessible at any number of remote stations —currently at formidable costs, but eventually at reasonable costs as information system technology inexorably advances.

These new kinds of physical tools have, as an equally important companion, development in the creation of new concepts and procedures for their utilization; in the computer field these two phases of the same development are often referred to as hardware and software. As one software example from the library field, and one made practical by the advancing computer technology, citation indexing has been developed by Eugene Garfield and his associates as a promising addition to library retrieval procedures.[7] As another software example made possible by advances in computer technology, mechanized information-dissemination schemes like the one developed by H. P. Luhn at IBM represent a way to bring records to the attention of the user on a selective basis.[8] These relatively simple software developments, and the more complex one of King for mechanical language translation, at least demonstrate a real potential for the software approach to information retrieval and dissemination.

[6] International Business Machine Corporation Research Center, *Final Report on Computer Set AN/GSQ—16 (XW—1)* (prepared under the direction of Gilbert W. King for Intelligence Laboratory, Rome Air Development Center [ARDC], Griffiss Air Force Base, New York. Contract AF30 [602]-1823. [RADC-TR59-110]. [6 vols.; Yorktown Heights, N.Y.: IBM, 1959]).

[7] Eugene Garfield and I. H. Sher, "New Factors in the Evaluation of Scientific Literature through Citation Indexing," *American Documentation,* XIV (1963), 195–201.

[8] H. P. Luhn, *Selective Dissemination of New Scientific Information with the Aid of Electronic Processing Equipment* (Yorktown Heights, N.Y.: IBM, 1959).

Case studies of successful library systems-engineering projects are not yet available, with a few minor exceptions, but these should be used eventually as a regular part of the library school curriculum. Meanwhile, systems engineering studies in other fields can substitute well to give the students a practical understanding of this discipline. Similarly, reports of major system-management efforts, as for weapons-systems projects like the Polaris missile development, can be used as case studies to acquaint the library student with techniques and concepts that are important for the successful prosecution and management of complex systems planning and development efforts.

We shall turn from systems-engineering methodology to close with a discussion of sample topics worth consideration for inclusion in the library curriculum, as suggested directly by our sample of social, political, and technological assumptions. Others are dealing with these problems in much greater depth than would be appropriate as a part of our discussion of the systems approach, but we are behaving in accordance with our definition of this term when we feel free to include any aspect whatsoever of the entire topic in our over-all systems analysis. It is a primary characteristic of the systems approach that it is circular, in the sense that early analysis of a complex systems problem may generate a requirement for much deeper study or research to be done by appropriate specialists, with their new findings and results to be used later in the systems approach to achieve a greatly improved solution.

Engineering interpretations of our social and political assumptions would be based upon knowledge of economic and social effects of alternatives for information publication and distribution, taxation and other means of financing library development and operation, and transition to modernized systems. For example, what governmental subsidies and support are necessary for the encouragement of the most desirable balance between privately operated libraries and those under direct governmental control? Or, what would be the net social and economic gain to the nation due to the implementation of some specific proposal for library development, such as the one made in the King team report? Or, what are the immediate practical implications for a major university library system, including possible impact on its building program, of an apparent trend toward computer-aided tutorial instruction as a supplement to traditional classroom programs? Certainly library schools should offer opportunities for some of their students to delve deeply into subjects relevant for consideration of questions such as these. Many of these courses must be taken outside the library schools, but specialties within the library school should be offered immediately for graduate students wishing to stress systems engineering or the systems sciences in their degree programs.

Engineering interpretations of our technological assumptions would be based upon knowledge of software and hardware advances in every relevant area of science and technology. For example, what are the possibilities for significant advances in the art and science of indexing, information retrieval, associational memories, linguistic standardization, computer-aided tutorial interaction, self-adaptive information dissemination procedures, and regional or national interlibrary communication nets—and what effect does this have on plans for acquisitions, new buildings, or other aspects of library development at each level of complexity?

I hope that my examples of library courses needed for students interested in the systems approach to library planning have illustrated the kind of intellectual content needed in the curriculum, whether or not it is all within the library school, if this approach is to be developed and used successfully by the library profession. Obviously, no student will be able to take all of these courses, but each must specialize in some limited aspect of library systems engineering.

As a closing remark, I note that the library systems-engineering curriculum will obviously be enriched materially by results of library systems research completed during future years. As with other professional fields, such as medicine or engineering, progress in research supports and enriches the educational process. Library schools, and the library profession generally, urgently need to expand their research programs greatly to include fundamental research in the system sciences relevant to library problems. Research results will provide the intellectual foundation for future education of library systems planners.

THE DEVELOPMENT OF A METHODOLOGY FOR SYSTEM DESIGN AND ITS ROLE IN LIBRARY EDUCATION

ROBERT M. HAYES

It is indeed a pleasure to participate with such distinguished company in this conference, which has a tradition behind it of leadership to the profession. I feel therefore compelled to issue a word of caution regarding what I shall say. It would be all too easy to conclude from my comments that information science (or system design as its most evident component) is to be viewed as the central purpose of library education. I do not regard it so. The tradition in library education is an honorable one, with meaning to this generation of librarians and to the ones to come. Information science may well affect that tradition; it will certainly interact with it, but it will never replace it. Please therefore regard my comments as presenting an addition to library education, not a substitute for it. With that background, let me now consider methodologies, system design, and library education.

INTRODUCTION

There is every indication that library education is undergoing a minor revolution and experiencing the addition of curriculums requiring new and radically different ranges of backgrounds, concepts, and approaches. In fact the change is evidenced by the very title of Area II of this conference: "Systems Planning and Analysis." In a very real sense, it is the concept of *system design* which has come to represent the revolution—it is probably the crucial concept in the theory and application of "information science." It is my personal belief that information science will become an integral part of library education, that it will become an increasingly important part of the librarian's professional and operational responsibility, and that it represents the theoretical, if not scientific, foundation of librarianship.

These things have all been said before, but of course that does not make them so. My intent here today is to demonstrate them as thoroughly and in as much detail as I possibly can. Before doing so, however, there are a number of crucial concepts which I should discuss or, where possible, define. Many of them were raised in the introduction to this conference.

First of all, what is "system design"? It is an approach, a process, a philosophy. It is based on the application of mathematical models to complex situations. It is oriented to the analytical study rather than the case study. It therefore approaches a complex situation by defining its component parts and representing their interrelationships by a relatively abstract model. It uses the model, rather than "similar" existing real situations, to help determine what a desired system should be.

I have said that system design is the crucial concept in information science. What then is "information science"; how does it differ from "information technology" and "library science"; how does it differ from "information specialty"? As I have said, it is a theoretical discipline, one which is concerned with the application of mathematics, system design, and other theoretical concepts to formalization of the processes in handling information. It is concerned with information technology but is in no sense identical with it. In fact, the tendency to identify the two is an unfortunate one, I think, since it has confused the true nature of information science. However, information technology—computers, micro-recording, communication systems—*has* represented the catalyst and made it so important to develop now the concepts of information science. On the other hand, "library science" has become almost completely identified with a specific type of information system and is, I feel, highly oriented toward the operational particulars of existing libraries. If this view is valid, then information science is the theoretical discipline of librarianship and library science is the professional one. Finally, the term "informational specialist" has sometimes been used as synonymous with "information scientist" and has led to confusion in the definition of the educational requirements for two very different types of need. I use the term "information specialist" to describe someone concerned with the operational utilization of a particular information system to meet the needs of the people served by it.

This leads me to a somewhat less evident question—or at least less often raised. Should information science be identified solely with the theoretical foundations of librarianship or, if it has wider meaning, what should be its relationship to education for other types of information systems? I think the answer is that information science has *very* broad meaning, encompassing the foundations not only of libraries but of business information systems, technical information systems, socio-economic data banks, and military command and control systems as well. Information science is most closely related to librarianship because of the traditional concern of librarianship with the more or less mechanical processes of information handling. However, students in business administration, engineering, and social science, interested in information systems in their respective areas, might well include courses in information science in their educational program, just as students preparing for professional library careers may. In addition, however, I think it is important for library schools to recognize that they have a responsibility to these other users of information systems. The responsibility is completely comparable to that which they have to the humanities, with the university research library, and the sciences, with the special library and information center.

In summary, information science is a theoretical discipline with broad application and with system design as its core concept. Since the concern of system design is the analysis of complex situations and the application of theoretical models to them, education for it must present the methodologies involved.

THE ROLE AND NATURE OF METHODOLOGIES

So, what do I mean by methodologies? They are those tools—intuitive, heuristic, procedural, mathematical—by which a new library environment or information requirement can be analyzed and an adequate information system developed to serve it. In one sense, this is very close to the work of the documentalists. Specifically, they have *actively* concerned themselves with analyzing new situations and with developing new systems; in doing so, they must have, consciously or unconsciously, used methodologies. In another sense, though, the documentalists have been quite far removed from the development of methodologies, since their concern has been with answering specific needs, not with how they arrived at the answers.

As a result, if methodologies for system design are to be developed, we must use the work of the documentalists not as examples of methods but as case histories to be studied for the methods used. In many examples, this is particularly easy, because the solutions they have proposed have been "pure"—and as a result probably ineffective—exemplifying not a solution but a method for getting a solution. In these cases, the documentalist has confused the "answer" with a particular way of getting answers, but for our purposes has made it easy to see what that way is.

Before discussing specific examples of methodologies and how to develop them, let me make some preliminary comments on their implications for library education. It amounts to this: my impression of library education, as it now exists, is that it is concerned with professional needs, with *particulars*, with techniques *as they are used in existing library environments*. If questions are raised in the educational process, they are answered in terms of those environments and, in fact, of the solutions which have already been selected. The result, at the worst, is the education of a set of well-trained clerks, familiar with all of the rules and all of their exceptions, able to fit into any existing library situation, but unable to adjust to a new one. At the best, the creative minds will be able to remold the solutions developed in the past, will be able to adjust them better to meet a new environment, but in doing so will be constrained to the familiar paths.

Unfortunately, this kind of education, while it may—in fact, does—very well meet the needs of the public library, completely fails to meet the needs of new information environments or the needs of growth in understanding of the library profession itself. Metcalfe[1] said, "Librarians are not without blame in having degraded cataloging and classifying . . . to fixed techniques or routines, in having allowed so much to be identified with the popular library and its simple needs." It is wider needs which the development of a methodology for system design hopes to meet. Through a critical examination of how solutions are developed, we educate personnel in the general foundations on which any solution can be developed.

Now, am I implying that without this type of foundation librarians cannot operate libraries or that system designers cannot design new systems? Certainly not. In fact, it is not even clear that such education will produce "better" librarians or system designers. It is clear, however, that we are dealing with an increasingly complex world and that the problems which librarians and system designers face are correspondingly complex. If they are to cope with them, they must have sophisticated, objective, well-defined tools to do so.

---

[1] John W. Metcalfe, *Information Indexing and Subject Cataloging* (New York: Scarecrow Press, 1957).

To pursue this last point further, I think it is evident from history that each generation, each person in fact, learns anew the lessons of the past. At a superficial level, it would appear that we learn nothing new, that the fundamental truths are ever the same. But it must be recognized that in each successive cycle, although the truths may be the same, the context is different, the structure of it is more complex, the problems in it are larger. It is this which forces us to learn anew, because the fundamental truths are really abstractions and the problem each generation faces is precisely that of seeing these abstractions in totally new situations, and usually in more complex ones.

Perhaps an analogy is appropriate. The design of a bridge is a difficult engineering job, but one which has been done, in one way or another, for hundreds of years. And the bridges designed, say, five hundred years ago were adequate not just for their times; some of them still stand and are in use today. Yet their design did not involve the use of abstract stress and vibration equations; the experience and intuition of the designer were all that were needed. Why then have such equations been developed? Why are they taught to engineers? Why are they used in the design of modern bridges and in what way are they used? And are they infallible guarantees against failures? The answers to these questions are, I think, almost self-evident; and they apply equally well if we raise the same questions with respect to the design of information systems and to the development and use of methodologies. Why should methodologies be developed, just as stress and vibration equations have been? Because they increase our understanding of the world and make explicit the criteria by which the competent creator uses his intuition and experience. Why should methodologies be taught, just as mathematics is taught to engineers? Because in this way the knowledge of the past can be communicated most readily, most objectively, and most concretely. Why should methodologies be used and in what way should they be used? Because they make evident the design considerations which must be considered and they describe the known relationships. But since they can only describe the relationships which have been formalized in them, they should be used as an aid to design, as a tool, not as a substitute. And are they infallible guarantees against failure? Obviously not! A "Narrows Bridge" collapses because the wind effects were not properly considered; doubtless there will be examples of information systems which fail despite the fact that well-defined methods were used in their design. But without the stress and vibration equations we could not even have considered constructing such a bridge, failure or not, and I think the time is near when we cannot consider designing information systems as complex as the world demands without methodologies.

Even at the very simplest of levels, consider the situation for a graduate, perhaps with two or three years of operating experience, who is in one way or another faced with the installation of a new library or information center. Recognize the problems he is faced with:

He is working under a very limited budget, perhaps just himself and a clerk. Should he use the organization's data-processing equipment to supplement the limited help? Perhaps he can use it without cost; in fact, using it may even strengthen his own position. What should he have the equipment do?

He is working in a relatively undefined information environment—no acquisition policies, no source definition, no prescribed services, little knowledge of the needs of his clients. How should he develop policies, sources, services? How does he determine the needs of clients?

He is working in a highly specialized field for which no established glossary exists and for which standard classifications are not adequate. How should he develop a glossary and classification adequate to the specialized needs and yet well controlled and compatible with broader ones?

He has no well-defined criteria for indexing, for file organization, and for all the other technical processes he must install. How does he do it?

It is clear that what we have defined are the problems of librarianship, whether we view them in the context of information systems, new special libraries, large research libraries, or the public library. Even for the librarian in an existing library, where his problem may be limited to the clerical aspects of library operation and whether to automate them or not, the librarian is faced with many questions for which he has no tools for assistance. If he is further faced with such problems as change of classification system, or addition of new fields of interest such as technical information for small business and industry, or similarly complicated professional problems, the lack of tools becomes almost embarrassing.

THE METHODOLOGIES OF SYSTEM DESIGN

Let me now be somewhat more explicit and describe the areas in which methodology development is now, at least implicitly, under way. I want to do this first by defining seven general areas and then by discussing two of them in detail.

First, the area of user study: What methods have been developed for defining the purposes and needs of the user, for specifying the services to him? For example, how should acquisition policies be determined? Some efforts have been made at developing questionnaires, others at using statistics, others at introducing "feedback."

Second, the area of vocabulary development: What methods are there for defining, structuring, and improving or updating the vocabulary? Since I will be discussing this particular area in detail, let me save further comments on it until later.

Third, the area of technical details of internal system processes: What methods exist for designing the formats of input records, file items, and output reports, for programming and flow-charting of operations? Here, the field of data-processing has been even more concerned with the need for methodologies and has developed techniques such as Gantt charts, matrix representations of systems, specialized languages, forms design. Most of them are equally applicable to comparable problems in information system design. As a result, the clerical type of problem, being closest to business data-processing, is almost certainly the most amenable to analysis and perhaps mechanization.

Fourth, the area of file organization: What methods exist for defining the physical structure of files? For example, what objective criteria are there for determining when to establish a branch library and what to put into it? I feel that this is a particularly important problem area, but one which has been much neglected in most of the considerations of the documentalists, probably because it arises only when we are concerned with very large files, too large to be linearly scanned. One approach has been the use of activity data, another has been the duplication of the structure inherent in the vocabulary, a third has been the use of *a posteriori* associations. I will use this as my second illustrative area and discuss these methods in detail.

Fifth, the area of the intellectual problems in judgment of relevancy and screening of material: What methods are there for determining the criteria or heuristics for matching patterns? Expressed in this way, it should be evident, even to the data-processing enthusiasts, just how complicated a problem we face. Methods for developing such heuristics will almost certainly be a long time in coming.

Sixth, the area of component (such as equipment) and system evaluation: What criteria are there for measuring performance and cost? For example, can "quality" be measured? Some cost-effectiveness models have been defined and the data-processing specialists have methods well in hand for both qualitative and quantitative evaluation.

Seventh, the area of organizational relationships: Are there methods for determining the optimum relationship between library and user, or library and management? These are problems with which modern business has struggled for years; the methods of organization theory are precisely those involved.

We tend to identify the solutions in many of these areas with techniques from the physical sciences, engineering, and business. But I must point out that they are equally relevant to the humanities. In fact, much of humanistic research is aimed at the most complex, ill-formulated aspects of them. I tend to view arts and letters as lying at the far end of the spectrum of creativity—at the very fringe of man's knowledge of himself and the world, at the most difficult level of making order out of chaos.

In summary, then, there are several areas in which methods either are being developed or are needed. For some, the methods can, at least in part, be drawn from cognate methods in other disciplines; for others—particularly vocabulary and file organization—the problems are central to librarianship and the methods must be developed by librarianship itself; for others—particularly the intellectual problems—the underlying difficulties are so great that their resolution will be a long time in coming, and our debt will be to the humanities for them.

METHODOLOGIES FOR VOCABULARY DEVELOPMENT

To illustrate the nature of methodology development as I am trying to explicate it here, let me discuss the methodologies for vocabulary development in detail. The problems in vocabulary development are those which have been central ones to librarianship and documentation: How do we derive appropriate words for document description? How do we define them, particularly in terms of their relationship to one another? How do we impose a structure on the set of them?

I ask these questions not because they are new ones, but because I intend to propose a new approach to them—to view the work which has been done for their solution in a somewhat different way, to discuss the work done on vocabulary development in terms of the *methods* which it has provided.

Consider, then, the methods for derivation of appropriate terms: first, we can call on some existing authority, such as the indexes to journals of the field or existing glossaries. Such an approach is, of course, of particular value in establishing an initial vocabulary. However, some workers have questioned this, and even if we recognize its value, it merely begs the question. Therefore, second, we can call on the documents themselves to generate their own terms.

In discussing the methods—statistical[2] and conceptual[3]—for deriving information-bearing words from texts, I am not here concerned with their use in indexing the source documents themselves. Rather, I am concerned with their use as the first step in constructing a subject authority. The aim is to determine what words are used in the field of interest, as exemplified in a particular document. They may or may not adequately describe the information content of the document itself.

Now, many of the projects concerned with this type of methodology have stopped at this range—usually with the intent of using the particular words from the particular document as descriptive of it. The permuted title index[4] is the most obvious example, but the statistical extract and some approaches to co-ordinate indexing are others.

The inadequacy of the vocabulary resulting from simply this first step is immediately evident to anyone using a permuted title—or permuted key word—index. The lack of organization, or even of cross-references, forces the user either to scan through the index or to generate the necessary term associations himself.

The second step, therefore, is to introduce those elements which convert a simple word list into a true subject authority: definitions and scope notes, references and cross-references, class relationships and analytic ones. What methodologies do we have here? There are many mechanical aids which can be drawn on to assist the subject specialist. The permuted index and the concordance, by bringing together the different contexts in which a word or phrase appears, by showing the types of associations, can aid the subject specialist in recognizing relationships. This has been extended in the form of the "semantic map"[5] which pictures the extent to which words have been associated in common. Presumably this statistical strength of association is based on an underlying semantic one.

Furthermore, there are many specific notations developed for representing the considerations involved in a subject authority. I have in mind those of the Western Reserve system,[6] of the

---

[2] H. P. Luhn, "A Statistical Approach to Mechanized Encoding and Searching of Literary Information," *IBM Journal of Research and Development,* I (October, 1957), 309–17.

[3] P. B. Baxendale, "Machine-made Index for Technical Literature—an Experiment," *IBM Journal of Research and Development,* II (October, 1958), 354–61.

[4] H. P. Luhn, "Keyword-in-Context Index for Technical Literature" (papers presented at the 136th meeting of the American Chemical Society, Division of Chemical Literature, Atlantic City, N.J., September 14, 1959).

[5] Lauren B. Doyle, "Semantic Road Maps for Literature Searchers," *Journal of the Association for Computing Machinery,* VIII (October, 1961), 553–78.

[6] J. W. Perry, A. Kent, and M. M. Berry, *Machine Literature Searching* (New York: Interscience, 1956).

Engineer's Joint Council,[7] of the Colon Classifications.[8] While in themselves these do not represent methodologies, they do provide an indication of the factors considered significant.

Again, many systems stop at this second step and assume that the subject authority—the thesaurus in some systems—is sufficient. However, even this has limitations and usually some attempt is made to impose a structure on it. We therefore come to one of the most fruitful aspects of methodology in the area of vocabulary development. I will discuss these methodologies in a sequence from the most complex intellectually to the most mechanistic.

First, simply to set the one end of the spectrum, we have the purely intuitive approach to classification, the organization of a field of knowledge—including its vocabulary—based solely on a view of what is "rational." The methodologies are the classical ones of taxonomy.

Second, there is a methodology, implicit in some of the models of vocabulary structure, which has not been exploited and represents an area of potentially fruitful research. Specifically, the vocabulary structure described by semantic relations among words has been represented by a *lattice,* and some recent work has indicated that in fact it is a distributive lattice.[9] It is a theorem of lattice theory that a distributive lattice can be decomposed—I use the term in its mathematical sense—into the direct product of elementary lattices in a unique manner. As a result, each word in the original lattice can then be represented, in terms of its position relative to each of the set of elementary lattices, as an ordered array. In this way, the inherent structure of the vocabulary is not disturbed but rather is displayed in a simple form, easy to grasp. This is an exact description of a vocabulary which has been facet-analyzed, and the mathematics of lattice decomposition should therefore be a model of the process of facet analysis.

Third, there is the methodology for structuring a vocabulary which is exemplified by the *filing rules* of the subject catalog. To the extent that such rules are formalized, they impose a sequence on the vocabulary designed to bring together those terms which are related, although the result is a structure only in a local sense.

Fourth, there are the several approaches which start from the premise, already mentioned, that semantic structure is derivable from statistical associations among terms as they are used together. These seek to decompose—again in the mathematical sense—the matrixes which describe the degree of association among terms. Whether the technique is factor analysis,[10] eigenvalue analysis, clumping,[11] or latent-

[7] B. E. Holm and L. E. Rasmussen, "Development of a Technical Thesaurus," *American Documentation,* XII (July, 1961), 184–90.

[8] S. R. Ranganathan, "Colon Classification and Its Approach to Documentation," in *Bibliographic Organization,* ed. Jesse H. Shera and Margaret E. Egan (Chicago: University of Chicago Press, 1951).

[9] Donald J. Hillman, *Study of Theories and Models of Information Storage and Retrieval* (NSF Grant No. G24070) (Bethlehem, Pa.: Lehigh University, 1962).

[10] Harold Borko and Myrna Bernick, "Automatic Document Classification," *Journal of the Association for Computing Machinery,* X (April, 1963), 151–62.

[11] A. F. Parker-Rhodes and R. M. Needham, *The Theory of Clumps* (Cambridge: Cambridge Language Research Unit, February, 1960).

class analysis,[12] the approach is pretty much the same. The only real differences lie in the particular choice for the measure of association.

Fifth, there is an approach which has masqueraded under a variety of names—"Scan-Column Index" of John O'Connor and Claire Schultz,[13] "Multi-List" of Prywes and Gray[14] at the University of Pennsylvania. More or less the methodology simply develops groups of terms by assigning each term to a group whose existing members have never been used with it. In this way, a single field can be assigned to all terms in a group without fear of overlap. The result may be a weird sort of structure, but perhaps not. In fact this methodology is implicit in all fixed field format item records, although, of course, one would not normally consider deriving them in so mechanical a fashion.

METHODOLOGIES FOR FILE ORGANIZATION

Strangely, the area of file organization has been remarkably neglected as one for study by the documentalists. In fact, only the data-processing specialists, concerned with the effective utilization of mass-storage media, have devoted any analytical attention to it. Yet, as I have indicated, this area is as central to librarianship as that of vocabulary development and control.

I think the comparative neglect is due to the tendency to identify file organization with vocabulary organization, to consider that physical organization necessarily reflects the intellectual one. This view is such a superficial one that some basic problems in file organization have been obscured and neglected. Since it has been an area of particular concern to me, I would like to review two of the problems in it and corresponding methodologies which have seemed crucial.

The first problem arises from the underlying economic reason that file organization is essential to the handling of large files: it is impossible to consider scanning through the entire file, looking for desired items or information; we must therefore select, on the basis of some simple criterion, a relatively small set of items which can then be examined more deeply. The first problem is then, evidently, the development of a suitable structure by which to provide a mechanism for successive screening. Do any methods exist by which the development of this mechanism, this indexing structure, can be aided?

The obvious one is that which in fact has obscured the difference between vocabulary structure and file structure: use the structure of the vocabulary—the subject headings, the class numbers, the key words. The advantage of this method is its relative ease and simplicity; it is a familiar approach, and therefore one which anyone can understand. Superficially, it appears that this *is* the criterion for organization in virtually all libraries.

In fact, however, there is another

---

[12] F. B. Baker, "Information Retrieval Based on Latent Clan Analysis," *Journal of the Association for Computing Machinery*, IX (October, 1962), 512–21.

[13] Claire K. Schultz and John J. O'Connor, "Designing More Efficient Indexes," *UNESCO Bulletin for Libraries*, XIV (July–August, 1960), 160–63, 191.

[14] N. Prywes and H. J. Gray, "The Organization of a Multi-List Type Associative Memory," *Proceedings of the Session on Gigacycle Computing Systems at the AIEE General Winter Meeting, January 1962* (AIEE Publication S-136), pp. 87–107.

method for file organization which has been used, almost unconsciously, to an equal extent. This is the method of "activity" organization, and much of my own work has been devoted to understanding this approach.[15] In brief, the method is based on the concept of making readily available those items in the file which are *likely* to be used. Of course, this begs the question of what is meant by "likelihood of being used" and of how it might be measured. Recognizing the difficulties, however, we must also recognize that there are many criteria, virtually any of which may have deficiencies but will be pragmatically adequate. The real question is how to derive a file organization from the one chosen. The approach I have adopted can be pictured as a "nested-box" structure, each of the boxes available at a given time having, ideally, an equal likelihood of being used. The result of this approach might be to make a single well-used book as available—both physically and intellectually—as large categories containing many books.

A third approach is a much more speculative one. It bases the organization on the similarity of items and groups together items which are similar to one another. Again, this too begs a question: How is similarity to be determined? It is this question which makes the method so speculative; however, it should be recognized that organization by subject or class number really represents the use of a simple measure of similarity—concern with a common subject—so as we extend our knowledge of the intellectual concepts of relevancy, we should correspondingly extend our concepts of file organization.

Let me now turn to the second problem, the one which arises from the *existence* of a file organization. The user of it is faced with a sequential decision process in which he successively selects sets of file items and index terms on the basis of some criterion of likelihood of finding the items of interest to him. The problem arises, of course, because there is no certainty that the items have been indexed or physically placed where he anticipates they will be. He must therefore use the clues provided by the indexing structure as part of a general strategy of search.

Since this is precisely the problem faced by the *reference* librarian, one method for developing a suitable strategy of search is to study the behavior evidenced by the operating reference librarian. The result of such study would be a set of protocols, or procedure descriptions, embodying the heuristics entering into successful sequential decision processes in file search.[16]

A radically different approach lies in the development of a general theory of indexing structures based upon the philosophy, if not the details, of communication theory. In fact, the concept of *sequential decoding*, if properly modified, provides an almost exact description of the processes of sequential decision making in search of a file.[17] To use this approach, we must characterize the "information content" of a file item or index entry and adopt a strategy designed to minimize search effort subject

[15] J. Becker and R. M. Hayes, *Information Storage and Retrieval: Tools, Elements, Theories* (New York: John Wiley & Sons, 1963), pp. 385–90.

[16] G. Carlson, *Search Strategy by Reference Librarians, Part 3 of the Final Report on the Organization of Large Files* (NSF Contract No. C-280) (Sherman Oaks, Calif.: Hughes Dynamics, Advanced Information Systems Division, March, 1964).

[17] J. M. Wozencraft and B. Reiffen, *Sequential Decoding* (New York: John Wiley & Sons and MIT Press), 1961.

to limiting the probability of "error"—that is, of missing desired items.[18] The penalty in any such screening process is that, as the probability is made smaller, the screening process must be made coarser, with a corresponding increase in the number of items which must be examined. The advantage of the sequential decoding approach is that the relationship between the probability of error and the cost of the screening process can be quantified and used as a design criterion.

ROLE OF METHODOLOGIES IN LIBRARY EDUCATION

Now my intent in reviewing with you this rather tedious list of methods for developing, defining, and structuring a vocabulary and a file is to demonstrate the extent to which methodologies exist. I now want to use the areas of vocabulary development and file organization to illustrate to what extent methodologies can enter into library education.

For example, the subject authority provides the threads by which the user can be led through the labyrinth of the library. If the student is to understand its importance, I think it is vital for him to know how it was constructed, what methods went into developing its system of references and cross-references, what underlying phenomena of the world it was intended to describe. If he is to be able to develop subject authorities for new situations, it is even more important for him to have these methods at his command.

The relationship between the subject authority and the subject catalog exemplifies a level of structure. The relatively well-defined rules by which the catalog is organized must be understood by the student. But in my mind it is not sufficient simply to call on the wisdom of the promulgator of those rules; he may well be right, but the student will understand better if he knows how and why the rules were made as they were.

The relationship between subject-cataloging and classification is a crucial one: it affects all of the processes of the library and its users. If this relationship can be objectively defined to the student—whether by the methods of taxonomy, lattice decomposition, or facet analysis—it becomes that much easier to communicate and learn. On the other hand, if it remains a subject of metaphysical authority or intuitive debate, the student is faced with regenerating all the principles himself.

Because the problems in file organization, particularly those involved in strategy of search, relate so closely to the work of the reference librarian, an understanding of search methodologies should have great significance to his education. The use of search protocols as model procedures, for example, can present search strategy in a clear-cut, well-defined manner. Such a programmed approach to education has been successful in many cases where it is important to follow procedures carefully.

In each case, understanding of a fundamental tool or principle of librarianship is enhanced if it is supported by understanding of the methodologies involved. I therefore feel it is vitally important that students in librarianship be introduced to the concepts and methodologies of information science.

---

[18] R. M. Hayes, *Measurement of File Operating Effectiveness—Time, Cost, and Information, Part 6 of the Final Report on the Organization of Large Files* (NSF Contract No. C-280) (Sherman Oaks, Calif.: Hughes Dynamics, Advanced Information Systems Division, April, 1964).

This does not mean that every librarian should become an information scientist. In fact I think it would be fatal to do so. Recognize that information science is a *theoretical* discipline, not a practical one or operational one. On the other hand, for system designers and researchers in the principles of librarianship, such education is essential.

In fact, the importance of information science to library education is most evident if we recognize the fundamental relationship between research and education. Why does the university place such strong emphasis on research productivity as the criterion for academic success, despite the pressures to recognize teaching ability as equally valid? I think there is a valid rationale: research productivity insures that as a *teacher* the individual will not become stale and trite, that he will continually be aware of the state of the art, not as an observer but as a participant.

I again recall for you the comment I quoted earlier from Metcalfe. Unfortunately, perhaps because of the overwhelming concern of library education with well-established professional particulars, perhaps because it has not developed a strong research orientation, library education *has* become stale and trite. Library schools have, until recently, been observers of the changes taking place in librarianship, not participants or, better yet, leaders of them. This is the real import which information science, as a research discipline, has for library education.

THE INFORMATION-SCIENCE CURRICULUM

For some time, there has been much discussion of what the nature of an information-science curriculum should be and how it should fit into the library school. Without pretending to know the answers, I would like to discuss some of the component parts of such a curriculum and some of the problems in it.

It is fairly easy to enumerate the areas of study which a competent information scientist should feel familiar with: mathematics, librarianship, engineering (particularly of data-processing equipment), linguistics, business administration, psychology, philosophy. You name it, and an argument can be found for its inclusion. The problems arise when we try to fit this into a normal year to year-and-a-half master's degree program, when we try to meet all the prerequisites.

In an effort to provide a reasonable rationale for the curriculum, I have divided it into four main areas: usage, operation, organization and design, and equipment. Courses are drawn from the disciplines of study enumerated above for their relevancy to these areas. Presumably the student in his undergraduate or MLS program has covered the requirements in one or two of the four areas. Therefore, his course of study should fill in his background in the other areas, perhaps extend his knowledge more deeply into the areas of his previous competence, and take the integrating courses which fit the four areas together into a total picture.

At UCLA we have defined three courses intended to fill this integrating role: "Data-Processing in the Library," a professional-level course designed to introduce the student to the nature of data-processing equipment and its application to various aspects—clerical, administrative, and intellectual—of library operation; "Information-System Analysis," a course oriented around the application of system-design methodology to the broad spectrum of information problems and designed to give meaning to the variety of courses from specific areas within the framework of information science; and "Problems in Information Science," a seminar course in development of methodologies for system design, intended to lead the student into independent study—and eventually research—of problem areas of information science itself.

SUMMARY

I feel that this talk has been remarkably diffuse, but perhaps that characterizes the problem. It has seemed necessary to define, as carefully as possible, the topic under consideration; to illustrate its diversity; to demonstrate its importance; to discuss its role in education. I have tried to do this in as much detail as is compatible with the existing state of development.

Let me summarize in as succinct and concentrated a manner as I can: the defining concern of information science is with understanding of the processes in handling and communicating recorded information. At the moment this is best achieved by concentration on the development of methodologies for system design, using the terms in the broad sense in which I have defined them. The results have importance not only in the obvious and relatively simple areas of improving clerical processes, but equally in all areas of professional librarianship. Perhaps most important, the introduction of these methodologies into library education should provide the students with greater understanding and prepare them better to use and extend the knowledge of the past. If the lessons of the past can be defined in an objective form, perhaps we can transmit them to the new generations without repeating the process of learning them by experience alone.

THEORETICAL PRINCIPLES OF INFORMATION ORGANIZATION IN LIBRARIANSHIP

VLADIMIR SLAMECKA AND MORTIMER TAUBE

LET us concur with the premise that the *raison d'être* of librarianship is "service." Leaving aside the less appealing servile meanings of the word, our premise implies that the objective of librarianship is not to create new and original knowledge, experience, and impressions of the mind and the senses; rather, it is to mediate such knowledge by facilitating its communication between and within individuals, societies, classes, and other echelons of mankind. This fundamentally social function of librarianship has, of course, important economic overtones.

The essence of library service has been described in terms of its "custodial" and "interpretive" functions involving, as fundamental activities and skills, the collection of certain records of human knowledge and work and their organization for storage and use. The justification of the library activities of collecting, organizing, and storing rests on the implied anticipation of use of these materials, although librarianship traditionally has not considered it its duty to generate the impetus for use.

The concept of library service is a changing one; it responds to quantitative factors as well as quality demands. In the course of time, the access services to the physical items have reached beyond the collection stored under the local library roof. Increase in volume of recorded materials has led not only to the development of co-operative acquisition projects and to a fine network of interlibrary loan channels. The heavy traffic in interlibrary loan, and the development of economical image reproduction and reduction techniques and media which again enable libraries to own comprehensive collections of materials regardless of volume, continue stressing local availability and access. On the horizon, however, are developments such as image telecommunication and even a partial replacement of the physical item by non-conventional information storing and sharing devices.

The symbolic representation of physical items—the access tool—has changed equally significantly. Interlibrary loan presumes the existence of adequate union catalogs in book form. Functional bibliographic control is so prodigious an undertaking that it, itself, cries out for organization; yet the planned practice of duplicating complete collections on microform and placing them in a relatively large number of libraries (as demonstrated by the library complex of the aerospace agencies and industry) lends an even greater importance to bibliographic control: today, indexed announcement lists or abstracting journals concomitantly serve as tools of access to the physical item and hence fully replace both the card or book catalog and the shelf list.

Many other examples of continuous change in the library service of providing access to materials could be cited; our aim is to show that librarianship is not a static profession. At the same time, the impetus for dynamic changes in service has not always emanated from within it. This is not unnatural: the development and growth of intellectual disciplines and professions depend, to an ever increasing degree, on interdisciplinary contributions. The main causes of such a development of intellectual disciplines, according to Abelson,[1] are twofold: the impact of new apparatus, and the application of techniques from one field to another. Both causes have certainly affected librarianship; the examples of the typewriter or the punched card and that of management analysis or systems design should suffice. On the other hand, the direct impact of librarianship on other professions or disciplines would seem to be of a lesser magnitude; this is also to be expected if we accept our premise that librarianship mediates knowledge rather than generates it and that its function stops there.

The enthusiasm with which a profession or discipline welcomes, examines, and exploits developments from other fields of human endeavor is a sign of its vitality, maturity, and self-confidence. This enthusiasm varies to some extent with profession and discipline: technical professions seem to develop more rapidly than the non-technical ones, and physical sciences with better-developed research methods change faster than social sciences. Whatever the reasons or their justification, the library profession has shown, historically, an uneasy rate of assimilation of changes emanating from outside its ranks. Emil Jacobs, it is said,[2] brushed off the then unconventional demands for information with the statement "Documentation? . . . They tell me industry needs it; if so, let it have it. But leave the libraries in peace with documentation"; he was neither accidental nor isolated in his attitude (even for Germany where the study of librarianship is traditionally concurrent with that of other disciplines). Librarianship appears to have then rejected an opportunity of assuming a more direct role in the exploitation of knowledge.

At the present time we are witnessing the establishment of a multidisciplinary profession called information technology and of a field of intellectual endeavor called (by some at least) theory of information systems. Their fundamental objective is to use current implements, intellectual and mechanical, to furnish the methods and systems for solving two areas of information service: a rapid and rational dissemination of information, and its long-term storage in a form in which it can be efficiently queried and retrieved. This objective must strike all librarians as differing from the professed services of the library profession only in the method it uses.

It is not our intention to add our ounce to the issue of whether librarianship includes documentation, or whether documentalists are information specialists who are special librarians who are librarians (or vice versa), or whether information technology is amateur, black-box librarianship; perhaps we may oblige all and regard ourselves as members of one large family. The crucial issue, from the viewpoint of the librarian family member, is that certain services, which historically seem to fall into the domain of the custodial and interpretive functions of his profession (either directly or by a logical extension of these functions), are performed outside the profession and, ad-

[1] P. H. Abelson, "Trends in Scientific Research," *Science*, CXLIII (January 17, 1964), 218–23.

[2] G. Leyh, A. Wilmanns, and E. Jacobs (eds.), *Festschrift Stollreither* (Erlangen: Universitäts-Bibliothek, 1950), p. 132.

mittedly, with some degree of success and a considerable degree of public acceptance.

It would also be shortsighted to deny the right of existence to new professions; today, the major influences at work in the realm of human endeavor lead to the development of multidisciplinary studies and skills—whether it is because the parent disciplines were unable to adapt their objectives or unwilling to amend their ways of thinking.

Our concern is that of finding for librarianship within this family of relatives a way of living and a fertile soil for healthy growing. We are concerned with the problem of discerning, assimilating, and putting to work judiciously the knowledge gained by those with whom we share, at least in part, common objectives but differ in the application of methods and techniques.

SUBJECT MATTER OF LIBRARIANSHIP

The process of development and growth is a synthetic one; the emphasis in it must lie, in the long run, on those factors which affect the basis of the profession, for these can expand or usurp its very existence.

The subject matter of librarianship, as that of other applied professions, falls into two categories. First, there is a body of formulated knowledge which underlies the outward manifestations of the profession. This is the "intellectual" content of librarianship: a cumulation of theories, propositions, hypotheses, relationships, and inferences formulated from experience. These are the "principles of librarianship," distinct from the philosophy of librarianship but essentially synonymous with its "theory," "elements," and "fundamentals," depending on how one chooses to interpret these concepts.

The second category of subject matter of librarianship is its "skills"—the several types of service rendered within the framework of the profession's objectives and functions. Parenthetically, they are either indigenous to the profession (such as those involved in the development of book collections, and the technical, reference, circulation, and advisory services), or sustentative of it (such as the organizational, managerial, administrative, and similar skills).

The degree to which a profession possesses a well-formulated body of underlying principles is indicative of its maturity; the degree to which a member of a profession understands and applies these principles determines the validity of his claim to professionalism. Above all, the development and formulation of principles are essential for the sustenance of librarianship as a profession. It follows that the principles are of fundamental concern to library education.

Before discussing principles which fall into the area assigned to us by this conference, several general observations on the relation of principles and skills are appropriate.

The formulation of principles underlying professions is usually an inductive process; that is to say, it follows chronologically their application. New skills and services often emanate from acute needs and thus have a pragmatic rather than theoretical rationale. The attempt at continuous formulation of principles remains, however, a property and mark of professions and disciplines.

A corollary of the inductive process of principle formulation is that the principles may be neither certain nor necessary; they are subject to change and further synthesis. As we know, some library skills and services are based on principles better defined than others; for example, principles underlying the cataloging skill differ from those of the advisory services in kind as well as in their degree of formality of formulation.

Finally, the concept of librarianship as an evolving profession implies that its skills and services change in time, as a result of pressures from within and without. It is true then that the body of knowledge which constitutes the intellectual foundation of librarianship is also subject to change, even though its overt services may remain essentially unaltered. For example: certain mechanical and semiautomatic methods of subject analysis—specifically, the technique of permutative subject indexing, coupled with automatic subject-heading assignment—are capable of implementing mechanically for certain types of materials the process of subject cataloging as a by-product of descriptive cataloging. Leaving aside the argument of product quality, here is a traditional library service performed in a radically different manner in which human subject analysis is replaced by a manipulation and matching of certain formally defined textual entities. The principles underlying the human and machine operations differ, yet the products—the subject catalog or index—are almost indistinguishable.

ASPECTS OF INFORMATION

Since known order is a prerequisite of access, organization may rightly be called a primary foundation of librarianship; without it, the profession would be without a rationale. The main object of organization in librarianship is "information"—the content of physical materials; this point was made from this platform four years ago,[3] and it needs no re-stating. For unless it is accepted that information is the proper object of library organization, with the physical item being a corollary of it, librarianship practically abrogates the interpretive function of its service. And if there is reality in recent prognoses[4] that all scientific information, with the exception of textbooks and certain monographs, will be distributed in the foreseeable future only in response to requests, what custodial function will there remain for the natural science, engineering, and many a special librarian?

Now information has been the subject of study of several disciplines; speaking broadly, philosophy, mathematics, linguistics, and engineering are all concerned with some of its aspects. The interest of philosophy is the truth, meaning, and interpretation of information; mathematics is concerned with the "statistical" behavior of information as signals devoid of meaning; linguistics with its structural configuration; and engineering is interested in the spatial manipulation of physical symbols which represent information. Librarianship, which handles physical materials in the engineering sense and their content in the logico-mathematical as well as the engineering and linguistic sense, must partake of the interests of all.

CLASS RELATIONS AS PRINCIPLES OF INFORMATION ORGANIZATION

Historically, this century has seen efforts to alter schemes of information order in two ways: by broadening their

---

[3] M. Taube, "Documentation, Information Retrieval, and Other New Techniques," *Library Quarterly*, XXXI (January, 1961), 90–103.

[4] V. A. Uspenskii and Y. A. Schreyder, "The Subject Matter of Scientific Information Theory," *Foreign Developments in Machine Translation and Information Processing*, CXLVI (December 18, 1963), 7–14.

scope and depth (as in the Universal Decimal Classification), and by removal of some of their structural constraints (as in faceted and, mainly, co-ordinate schemes). Among the reasons for the first development is the one cold fact amid the heated arguments about the significance of the exponential increase of knowledge: if the efficiency of access is to remain high, relatively constant, and independent of the knowledge-growth factor, the detail of organization must increase (although not linearly with that factor). The second development follows when we realize that for a given level of constraints to information access, an increase in detail of organization does not necessarily imply a concomitant increase in efficiency of access.

The impact of the co-ordinate schemes of order, which theoretically carried these developments farthest, was described in 1952 as follows:

> The value of this new approach to bibliographic classification as an instrument for the analysis and organization of literature is at once apparent when it is re-examined with respect to the limitations inherent in the traditional book classifications as they are generally employed in libraries. Since the analysis of literature in terms of its constituent thought units dissociates content from the physical object (book) the limitation of *linearity* cannot apply. Nor does the limitation of *inconsistency of organization* apply because it is a conceptual, rather than a book, classification and hence inconsistencies due to the physical nature of books do not have to be introduced into the system. Further, by denial of the principle of a universal classification and insistence upon individual and separate schematisms for each field, or segment of a field, of knowledge, internal consistency throughout any given scheme can be maintained. The limitation of *inherent incompleteness* is avoided and the system becomes *infinitely hospitable* because it is a referential, rather than a hierarchical structure, and thus can be expanded at any point without doing violence to an underlying hierarchy.

Finally it escapes *complexity* by being utilitarian and practicable rather than theoretical and hence is as simple as the field to which it relates and the purposes or objectives for which it is created. Its approach is pragmatic rather than absolute.[5]

Today it is apparent that these efforts have attained a broader significance: they appear to have indicated the necessary and sufficient factors of organization of information in librarianship and as such have laid an intellectual foundation to it. We submit that the two factors, or principles, are the *intellectual and the topological relation of classes of information*.

Regardless of the scheme of order we may think of for information, it will always contain at least two constraints. First, since random order is contrary to the essence of organization, each scheme must always define the location (i.e., the spatial position) of one entity or class in relation to another entity or class. Second, if meaning is an attribute extraneous to a class, theoretically no scheme can ever adequately define the intellectual relation between two classes a priori. The hypothesis that the two conditions of class relation, which we shall call here the "topological" and the "intellectual" relation (or the "physical" and the "conceptual" relation), are sufficient and necessary to define any scheme of order of information underlies their choice as the principles of information organization in librarianship.

In all non-manipulative schemes of information order, the absence of physical proximity of two classes is tantamount to a lack of intellectual relation

---

[5] J. H. Shera, "Classification: Current Functions and Applications to the Subject Analysis of Library Materials," in *The Subject Analysis of Library Materials* (New York: Columbia University, 1953), p. 39.

between them. One direction of effort in the history of library classification has been the attempt to identify certain predominant intellectual relations and to associate the related classes topologically (physically). The resulting so-called logical schemes, which largely exhibit the hierarchical relation between classes, suffer from the very reason that topological preference to one class relation precludes, or encumbers, the topological expression of another intellectual relation of that class.

Realizing the topological difficulty of reflecting in a scheme of order most of the real-world intellectual relations between classes, the co-ordinate schemes assume for each class an equiprobable chance of intellectual relations, and they proceed to arrange classes into a functionally optimum topological order—an alphabetical one.

To overcome (mainly) the limitations of "logical" arrangement, non-manipulative linear classifications loosen their rigidity by providing a topologically equivalent (alphabetical) index to their schedules. On their part, the multidimensional co-ordinate schemes overcome the absence of a physical link between intellectually related classes by the provision of a syndetic apparatus. It would indeed seem, as has been suggested, that we have but rediscovered Cutter, and that as manual tools of access, our schemes are not significantly different from each other in effectiveness. In reality, of course, there are significant differences, present and potential.

For instance, the basis of building the syndetic apparatus into the structure of co-ordinate schemes can differ from that employed in logical classifications, particularly in the manipulative systems. The invariable intellectual relations (that is, those which apply in all situations) apparently occur only at the subclass level, for example, between "tree" and "green tree," and they are by definition limited to inclusion or equivalence; these can be expressed as instructions. The remainder of intellectual relations between classes are all variable and hence permissive only; the criteria of their inclusion into the scheme, however, no longer need to rest upon educated guesses of lexicographers but become a matter of statistical choice, reflecting the real world.

The use of statistical criteria for selection of classes related massively by concept opens up the possibility of continuous optimization of the syndetic apparatus, and of information organization and retrieval. This task requires considerable computations and continuous comparisons, and it cannot be delegated to either the user, or the lexicographer, the cataloger, or the indexer. Furthermore, the human mind is not concerned with statistical significance but with a subjective one; it repeatedly invokes the personal viewpoint. Such optimization is a task of suitably programmed machines. In this sense, therefore, the optimum capabilities of co-ordinate schemes of order are exploited to their maximum only with the aid of such equipment. This is due to the compatibility of the class relation concept of co-ordinate schemes with the principles by which modern calculating machines operate.

In essence, present-day machines such as digital computers optimize the ability of co-ordinate schemes to overcome the constraint in non-manipulative schemes of having to express intellectual class relations by physical proximity. Machines are capable of seeking, identifying, and exploiting intellectual relations between classes on the basis of non-subjective criteria, when these are expressed as formal rules and brought to bear by programming. Hence the present-day emphasis upon formalization: it obviates the inconsistency as a result of which order loses some of its effectiveness and purpose. By the same token, machines can eliminate the need for a priori predictions of variable intellectual relations between classes.

However, just as they do not obviate the existence of intellectual relations, machines are not free from the topological constraint. Problems such as the choice between parallel and serial access—whether relating to book shelves or magnetic tape—are a consequence of our having to allocate and manipulate classes in a physical and temporal domain. Yet somewhere between these two constraints, the intellectual and the topological, we do make a choice or strike a balance.

We do so by employing certain criteria to judge the portent of the one constraint against that of the other. For example, in seeking to organize information for access, we employ the topologically most functional arrangement of classes in order to facilitate an optimum exploitation of intellectual class relations; we rate the latter more important than the topological ones. This need not always be the rule. Consider, for instance, a family of classes consisting of libraries instead of information: we would probably view their topological constraint (i.e., their geographic dispersion) more weighty than some of the non-physical relations and hence would abandon the idea of, say, co-operative acquisitions between Alaska and New Zealand.

Contained in our hypothesis of class relations is a maxim of prime importance: we must choose and apply our criteria in such a way that they pertain to the entire family of classes. If our family is information, that is, the intellectual content of physical records, we cannot seek solutions to the organization of information in books separately from solutions for periodicals, and for documents, and for patents, or for microfilm; this is because the criteria of importance applied to one group of classes almost certainly differ from those those of other classes. Only if we sought to order monographs as physical objects, and periodicals as physical objects, and manuscripts or microfilm as physical objects, without any concern for their content, could we consider them as separate families of classes, since then one family could conceivably have no classes in common with any other family. We can, and do, treat serial records separately from book records, for example.

This maxim can be shown to follow from our previous reasoning of the necessity and sufficiency of the two relations as conditions defining organization of information. We can expect a solution to be optimal for the whole family of classes and consistent for all its segments only if we can define that family of classes uniquely—that is, if it has no relation with another family. To put it differently, there must be a denominator common to all the classes of the family, and unique to that family.

This maxim has ponderous implications: it teaches that we must consider and undertake the problem of organization of information from the viewpoint of total library service, encompassing all information carriers and all services affected by the organization. And, by extension, it teaches that we should consider and undertake from the same "total" viewpoint problems other than organization of information; our family of classes need not be information but a complex of regional libraries, co-operative acquisitions, or a national network of information centers. This is, of course, what we mean by "systems approach," and why its methodology and application are so important in librarianship today.

THE PRESENT ROLE OF LIBRARIANSHIP

It would be a serious fallacy to assume that the abandonment of traditional methods of information organizing in favor of the empirical, statistical, and systems approach delegates the responsibility for the whole enterprise to information technology or the computer services. On the one hand, the library profession cannot avoid the impact of this development; the computer-compiled book catalog has made a strong entry already, and there is the distinct possibility of continuous automatic readjustment of intellectual class relations within its syndetic structure. For certain types of materials, subject analysis by machine already obviates subject cataloging, and it too is capable of continuous internal optimization in accordance with certain hypotheses of information theory. There is also evidence that the assignment of classes in a scheme of order can benefit from a statistical definition.

On the other hand, the library profession does have a significant contribution to make; were it not so, we should despair. It lies in at least two areas: that of the continuing formalization of class relations and criteria, and that of the verification and optimization of these formalizations via feedback from the outside world.

The search for formal relationships between entities and the evaluation of criteria of preference presume an acquaintance with the underlying principles governing them; the library profession is much suited to perform this synthesis. There are many aspects of the problem of intellectual access to information which merit and await our attention; dominant among these are those which are attributes of humans. As an example, consider the concept of human inconsistency as a factor in organization of information: Do we know its significance? Do we know it in all of its manifestations—in cataloging, classification, indexing, abstracting, paper-writing, title-writing, reference-citing, question-asking, and judging the relevance of answers? Or again, can we assign a maximum tolerance level to such criteria of design as inconsistency, or cost, or access time?

The search for a greater level of objectivity (formalization) in the problem of intellectual access to information results in our building of operating models; these need validation. The library profession has perhaps a better opportunity than any other homogeneous group to monitor the operation *on the outside*. The feedback from the outside must, however, be organized, not sporadic; and it must make a claim for validity. Again, both requirements presume an acquaintance with the underlying principles; furthermore, they presume a plan and a methodology.

A PRAGMATIC CORE OF LIBRARY EDUCATION

We have attempted to outline the principles upon which there appears to be founded one segment of library service—the organization of, and access to, information. Our intent was to identify and define these principles, not to elaborate them at this time as a full theory; we do suggest, however, that such a theory is possible and desirable.

To complete our assignment, it remains to allot this theory a suitable place in the subject matter of library school curriculums, and to prepare a systematic outline for class presentation.

The course outline suggested below is predicated on the position that organization of information is intrinsic and indigenous to librarianship and to its continuance. In contrast to the newer programs now being proposed for the education of information science or technology specialists whose profession at present appears distinguished from that of librarianship by the absence from its objectives of certain kinds of service, the education for librarianship must present the subject of intellectual and physical manipulation of information within the balanced framework of a well-proportioned curriculum catering to all the profession's obejctives. Within the thirty-six-credit-hour graduate program, the library curriculum will thus hardly find room for courses on probability, mathematical models of communication, linguistic analysis, metalanguages, or the design of switching circuits—except as a peripheral part of a doctoral curriculum. Library education should take the position that its interest in these subjects is satisfied at the level which furnishes the student with adequate knowledge to perform as a professional today and which assures his contribution to a healthy development of the profession tomorrow—and proceed to examine, or redefine, its objectives. Given its historical objectives, however, the attempts of some to make the present-day library curriculum predominantly mathematical or engineering in content are as unrealistic as the refusal of others to allow introducing into it such concepts of numeration, engineering design, and the rigor of scientific methods as are pertinent to the profession's continuing evolution.

The course outline suggested below seeks to offer a systematic, broad, and encompassing development of the subject of information organization in librarianship; unless the traditional subjects of classification and cataloging are presented in our schools with no other aim but that of turning out practitioners in the Library of Congress classification system and cataloging skill, the subject of information organization must be presented in a context within which *any* particular system, old or new, is a specific application of general principles.

The following areas form, in our opinion, such a context: the concept of "organization" as a function of library service, the concept of "information" in librarianship, and the concept of "formality" (formal relations) pertaining to the organization of information in librarianship. Given an understanding of these concepts and of their tools (mathematical, logical, mechanical, etc.), old and new solutions of the organization of library materials and information can be presented—as extensively or shallowly as desirable—in the light of applications of principles, techniques, and equipment.

A minimal curricular outline for the subject area of organization of information in librarianship is suggested below.

ORGANIZATION OF INFORMATION: A CURRICULAR OUTLINE

1. The concept of organization as a function of library service
    - Organization and access
    - Knowledge, physical materials, and information
    - Changing objects of organization in library service
    - Bibliographic organization
2. The concept of information in librarianship
    - Information as object of study of various disciplines
    - Attributes of information as constraints in its organization: intellectual and topological constraints
3. The concept of formal relations
    - Order, consistency, and formality
    - Algebra of classes, truth functions
    - Modern machines: principles of operation
    - Topological organization and manipulation of classes in machine: coding, file organization, sorting, matching
    - Machine language, algorithms, programming
4. Organization of materials and information: historical solutions
    - Symbolic representation of materials and information
    - Organization of physical materials: books, microfilm, etc.
    - Organization of access tools: catalogs, subject heading lists, bibliographies, indexes, thesauruses
5. Topological and intellectual relations of information classes: new solutions
    - Basic concepts and methodology
    - Formal criteria for subject analysis; limitations of human and machine applications
    - Formal criteria for derivation of conceptual relations; applications in cataloging, searching, indexing, retrieval
    - The systems concept of information organization; function, products, techniques
6. The role of the library profession: formalization, evaluation

LIBRARY EDUCATION: THE ROLE OF CLASSIFICATION, INDEXING, AND SUBJECT ANALYSIS

D. J. FOSKETT

I HAVE chosen my title with some care, in relation to the theme of this conference, because I wish to establish one particular point at the outset. I believe that the study of classification and subject analysis represents the intellectual zenith of education for librarianship; but it is not, for librarians, an end in itself. Librarianship is a practical activity carried on in circumstances that vary greatly, but the end is always the same: to provide readers with the books and information they need. Education for librarianship has for its object, therefore, the fitting of librarians to do this in the most effective way, according to the different circumstances in which they may operate. Techniques, however absorbing as an academic study, are no more than tools, to be used only as long as they prove able to do the work.

This conference is very timely; discussions on education for librarianship are taking place all over the world, and there is more interest than ever in the *professional* aspects. The recent issues of *Special Libraries* and *Library Trends* show that the relationship between vocational and academic exercises the minds of library educators to what is perhaps an unprecedented degree.

In this respect, the United States has led the world. Whatever dissatisfaction your leading librarians may express, from time to time, about the state of affairs in the library schools, your curriculums have always had a firm foundation in practical matters. You need only look at Wilhelm Munthe's glowing and well-deserved tribute to the work of the Chicago Graduate Library School, as long ago as 1939, to see how much this approach has been welcomed abroad.[1] Many of us regret deeply that we have as yet done so little to imitate it.

It is true that, in many other countries, education for librarianship has also been centered in the universities, but the result has not been the same. There has been a strong tendency for university courses to produce scholars who are primarily subject specialists concentrating on bibliography—particularly on historical bibliography. In other words, the emphasis has been almost wholly on the production of librarians who will work as academic staff in the continental-style universities. In the United Kingdom, we have had, until lately, an even worse situation. As you probably know, one of our amiable eccentricities has been to pretend that our universities exist for the education of gentlemen, who shall be well equipped to conduct elegant Socratic discourse, preferably in Greek, but who are under no particular necessity to labor for their daily bread. We have been inclined to overlook the fact that our universities had their origins as vocational-training establishments for theology, medicine, and law and to regard such training as something which has to be gained, if absolutely necessary, by courses at lesser institutions. I am glad to say that this attitude, if not yet quite dead, is at least

[1] Wilhelm Munthe, *American Librarianship from a European Angle* (Chicago: American Library Association, 1939).

moribund. But it has meant that most of our education for librarianship has been carried out first through part-time study, and since the war through full-time study, at local authority colleges with less than university status and with a very severely limited vocational bias. Until last year, only University College, London, offered a postgraduate diploma in the School of Librarianship and Archives. We are now busily engaged in some considerable reorganization of our higher educational system, and it is not unlikely that more universities will follow the example of Sheffield and Queen's, Belfast, both of which have recently established schools of librarianship.

Now tradition is a fine thing, so long as it is a living thing and does not overlay the needs of the present with the dead hand of the past. What we have to gain from our British university tradition, I think, is no less than the theme of this conference; that is, the founding of library education on basic principles and the establishing of a scientific discipline, something more than vocational training though closely allied to it. I am not yet sure whether we can find normative principles that can be distinguished as "laws" of library science, though Dr. S. R. Ranganathan, who only last month was honored by the University of Pittsburgh, has already proposed his own five laws;[2] and, if one defines a law as a general statement true in all particular instances, his propositions certainly have a claim to rank as such:

> Books are for use;
> Every reader his book;
> Every book its reader;
> Save the time of the reader;
> A library is a growing organism.

These are clearly different from, say, the laws of thermodynamics. But librarianship, we must remember, is a social science; it is not a natural science, or even a technology. It has a social aim—to serve people, not to produce objects. As Ranganathan has expressed it, "Library service to living men must at the ultimate stage be done by living men."[3] Our capital is intellectual; our dividends are measured in terms of human needs and fulfilment. We cannot expect to find our principles by investigation in the laboratory or even by exploring the profundities of mathematical reasoning. But we need techniques and systems to cope with the material we have to handle. The important thing is that these techniques should not be made ends in themselves but studied in relation to their social purpose. By this I mean that, while we retain a vocational element in our program of education, this should be regarded in a general light. We are fitting people to play a role in society, without limiting them to one particular social situation. Endless descriptions of the "how-I-run-my-library-good" type may be appropriate to in-service training but not to library education.

In this section of the conference we come to the "reference situation," the problems of intellectual access to information. Put in simple terms, a reader becomes conscious of a gap in his knowledge, formulates a question, and seeks an answer. I include under this heading both retrospective searching for information already published and information service based on current literature, even though the latter is based on the librarian's own knowledge of his reader's needs and not on specif-

[2] S. R. Ranganathan, *Five Laws of Library Science* (London: E. Goldston, 1931).

[3] S. R. Ranganathan, "Reference Service and Humanism," *Abgila*, I (March, 1949), 1–6.

ically formulated questions. To be prepared to give such a service, we have to know how questions arise.

Until the enormous increase in the quantity of research and publication that has taken place in the twentieth century, the normal approach to a library was by means of a known author. A scholar would probably know personally, and would certainly know by name, all the important people writing in his field. Scholar-librarians, having been through the same type of university courses, would react in a knowledgeable way to the inquiries they received, for they would be familiar with their background. In these circumstances, the questions asked would be for the works of specific, named writers or the publications of specific organizations known to be working in the field. The librarian's main piece of equipment for tackling this situation is the author catalog, and it is not surprising that great attention was paid in the nineteenth century to the establishment of codes of rules for consistent author headings. Even today, most British university libraries do not provide subject catalogs.

One of the great contributions of the public library movement, and particularly of the American public library movement, has been its insistence on the need for technical expertise. When libraries were provided for the general public, many of whom had no education in scholarship, it soon became clear that the librarians would have to develop methods for dealing with questions that were framed in another way, questions that had not been formulated in terms of known authors but were the simple expression of a need for information. Subject catalogs and bibliographies became necessary, and librarians came to need skill in making and using them. As long ago as 1869, that great English pioneer Edward Edwards wrote that "*any* really classified catalogue—however defective and assailable its theoretical system—cannot, in the nature of things, fail to assist and facilitate the researches of a really working reader and student, in a much greater degree and measure, than can the *best* conceivable catalogue arranged according to Authors' names."[4] At about the same time, Melvil Dewey was preparing to usher in a new era with his Decimal Classification, and shortly afterward began the battle for open access to the library shelves. It is certain that this could not have been won without the help of that great scheme by means of which books could be arranged on shelves in a way helpful to all readers, even those quite ignorant of any authors' names.

The same situation exists today. I have visited hundreds of libraries, and I see no sign of any decrease in the need for helpful order in the arrangement of documents and systematic catalogs to give readers a conspectus of the library's stock in the subjects of their interest. But in order to be helpful, these arrangements must keep up to date with both the progress of knowledge and the way in which knowledge is sought.

This is one aspect of the significance, in education for librarians, of classification and indexing theory. These are the tools we need for the arrangement of documents according to their subjects and for the choice of terms for indexes. They are not, emphatically not, to be confused with filing and sorting *devices,* however excellent these may

---

[4] Edward Edwards, *Free Town Libraries* (London: Trübner, 1869), pp. 5, 52.

be. The basic requirement is a matrix or set of terms, with means for expressing relations between terms, able to be arranged in a preferred sequence automatically fixed by a system of notational symbols. Each library has much in common with other libraries, so that the general principles of classification and indexing serve as a foundation study. But each library also operates in its own unique situation; it is clear, therefore, that the study must be extended into the details of designing and using schemes in relation to those situations. Every librarian must be equipped to devise, if necessary, a scheme uniquely suitable for his own place.

Reduced to its bare fundamentals, reference service means translating a need for information, as expressed by a reader, into an entry in a bibliography or a library catalog—matching one set of terms against another. This is a situation differing significantly from that of the scholar lookng in an author catalog; for when questons are put in terms of subjects, indexing must be in subject terms. But which terms? No document exists as a totally isolated unit, so that to rely wholly on each author's own terms may make difficulties. Every writer on a subject is trying to describe his conception of reality in relation to what is already known. This description, apart from those few subjects, like mathematics, with an agreed-upon symbolism, has to be in natural language, a notably inexact tool. The act of indexing or classifying is to relate each new subject-document to a scheme that has been established by its predecessors—by what is already in the collection. This means, of course, without relation to the document in hand.

The same applies to a subject inquiry—a point that is often overlooked. It is assumed that an inquirer is able to specify exactly what he wants in the terms used in the library's system. All experienced reference librarians know that this is rarely the case, that usually the inquirer has to be guided from a very general statement toward a more precise formulation of his needs. It is interesting to note that this has been confirmed by the recent comparative study, made by Cyril Cleverdon, of the efficiency of the faceted classification made for the Cranfield College of Aeronautics, and of the Western Reserve University semantic code index. In his acute analysis of the results of this test, Alan Rees points out that "consistency can greatly affect the performance of an indexing system" and that "the search results were greatly influenced by the lack of recourse to the questioner during question analysis." Rees further agrees with Cleverdon's statement that "Cranfield programs had better concept matching than WRU, omitting fewer concepts, adding fewer concepts, whether more or less specific than the question." And, most significantly, Rees states that, whereas "there is a close parity between language of authors, language of documents and indexing languages," this parity is far less in the reference situation, because "the language of questions represents in many cases an attempt to *form* and *define* concepts."[5]

Here we reach the problem lying at the very heart of information-seeking, and indeed of learning itself. How do we form concepts? If we knew this, we could design systems to reflect the process.

[5] Alan M. Rees, *Review of a Report of the Aslib-Cranfield Test of the Index of Metallurgical Literature of Western Reserve University* (Cleveland: Western Reserve, 1963).

In fact, we do know a fair amount about it, since a great deal of research has been carried out by experimental psychologists. Among the most notable work is that of Jean Piaget and his colleagues in the University of Geneva. Piaget has published a long series of important works, the latest of which, with Bärbel Inhelder, has particular relevance to the present discussion.[6] It is *The Early Growth of Logic in the Child,* a study of classification and seriation, and records observations on more than 2,000 children ranging in age from under two years to nine years. This work proves several things. It shows that the first and fundamental source of knowledge is action. The child comes into contact with various objects and begins to learn by performing certain actions which are quite elementary—piling, separating, putting into lines, and so on. He soon forms schemes of operations, from which he derives perceptual data which he then combines into groups—he begins to classify. Contrary to what one might expect, seriation does not appear long before classification; the two develop together. Both are essentially operational forms of behavior and the development of each is assisted by the development of the other. Identification of an object is bound up with its inclusion in a class: "This is an orange"—a combination of perceptual data such as color and shape, closely linked with sensory-motor schemata: peeling, chewing, and so on.

This notion of class inclusion, with the co-ordination of intension and extension, is achieved through actions which involve both hindsight and anticipation and leads to the recognition of properties. Two forms of action are involved, called by Piaget the "ascending" and "descending" methods. The "ascending" method, or synthesis, means the forming of collections of objects with common properties; the "descending" method, or analysis, means the separating of objects from a collection by their possession of special properties. These operations lead to the formation of additive or hierarchical classifications, of flowers and animals, for example, with complementary classes themselves being linked to form still larger groups.

Even more significant, perhaps, from our point of view is that, *at about the same time,* children learn to make multiplicative classifications or matrixes; they see that a collection of objects can be grouped into different sets on the basis of different characteristics, according to the purpose of the classification. We thus have convincing experimental evidence for the criticisms made of traditional Aristotelian classification as shown in the classificatory sciences and in the Decimal Classification—in which a genus was divided and subdivided into a single chain of dependent classes. These criticisms were well summarized by J. H. Shera, adducing the evidence of American psychologists, in his address to the Dorking Conference on Classification for Information Retrieval.[7] What has happened in these enumerative classifications such as DC is that the maker has tried to list all terms arising out of multiplicative classification in one se-

---

[6] B. Inhelder and J. Piaget, *The Early Growth of Logic in the Child: Classification and Seriation* (London: Routledge & Kegan Paul, 1964).

[7] J. H. Shera, "Pattern, Structure, and Conceptualization in Classification for Information Retrieval," in *Proceedings of the International Study Conference on Classification for Information Retrieval, Dorking, May 1957* (London: Aslib, 1957), pp. 15–27.

quence, thus producing a single series instead of a lattice system. The inevitable result is that we get complex subjects listed as if they were simple, one-aspect subjects. To quote an obvious example, the class 372.2 in DC, which is "Elementary-school organization," contains a mixture of types of school and curriculum subjects all in the same series of subdivisions. Thus the apparently one-aspect subject "Storytelling" at 372.214 actually means "Storytelling in the elementary school." There are two criticisms to be made of this procedure. First, the subject is not a species to its so-called genus: it is not a type of elementary school. Second, because "Storytelling" is given as a division of "elementary school," no provision can be made for a subject such as "Storytelling in the nursery school." "Nursery school" has a place, but there can be no link between it and "Storytelling."

As I said, this is an obvious example, but it illustrates clearly a major defect of traditional classifications, and one that becomes increasingly exasperating. Such classifications, because they are unable to form lattices, cannot classify complex subjects that were not foreseen by the maker of the scheme. This includes most of the reference questions asked today. Small wonder that reference librarians express dissatisfaction with classification and look for other means of providing keys to their collections.

Before exploring this point further, I should like to turn to another aspect of the learning process. We learn about phenomena through operational schemata, and our actions produce a series of signals caused by stimuli and their traces in the cerebral hemispheres, which directly affect the cells of the visual, auditory, and other receptor mechanisms. This primary signaling system is common to man and animals. Man, however, has a second signaling system, namely language, which is peculiarly his own. That this is secondary is shown by Piaget, who included a number of deaf children in his latest experiments; they were slower to learn but demonstrated both that they were able to learn and that their learning processes were the same as for hearing children. Piaget concludes that "research has proved that language accelerates the process of classification and seriation and helps to complete them." Through language man makes abstractions and generalizations of the primary signals and by analysis and synthesis of these generalizations forms a new structure—language—which enables him both to create and to transmit information.

This combination of analysis and synthesis, shown by Piaget to proceed together in concept formation, has also been stressed by Louis Hjelmslev, the leader of the Copenhagen Linguistic Circle.[8] In studying the nature of language, we do not begin with individuals and synthesize them into classes, as previous linguistics had assumed; we begin rather with the as yet unanalyzed text so that the only possible first step is to proceed from class to component, an analytic and specifying movement. Thus we now have a combination of the generalizing movement deriving from the primary signaling system and a specifying movement deriving from the secondary signaling system. The ascending and descending processes observed by Piaget in concept formation

[8] Louis Hjelmslev, *Prolegomena to a Theory of Language* (Madison: University of Wisconsin, 1961).

are repeated in the development of language itself.

It thus becomes even clearer that the enumerative classification scheme falls short both as a means for ordering concepts and as a system for combining symbols on the linguistic model. Even more does it fail as a mathematical system. I am not a mathematician, but fortunately many demonstrations of this inadequacy have been made in the pages of *American Documentation;* and in England we have had the benefit of the highly effective criticisms, with their entertainingly eccentric presentation, of Robert Fairthorne.[9]

If traditional library classification is based on a method which so clearly fails to cope with the structure of information both as it is recorded and as it is sought, what is the point of continuing to study it? If it is indeed true, as Dr. Taube[10] has suggested, that "standard library practice assumes that, in general, it is possible to express any specific topic in a single word or phrase," then the sooner we abandon such practice the better, because it is no longer possible to reduce the specific subjects of research in this way. Cutter was wrong when he stated that the subject expressed by the words "the movement of fluid in plants" is physiological botany; we may choose to say that this is a general name for the field in which the subject appears, but the subject itself is, of course, "the movement of fluids in plants." I was rather astonished to find the same procedure cropping up in the recent comparative tests on automatic classification by Harold Borko. In the SDC technical memorandum of October 18, 1963, terms found in a collection of documents dealing with computers were grouped into 21 categories, but these were not used as a lattice system, and "a document was classified into the one most relevant category only." This, to my mind, rather vitiates the whole test, and no doubt accounts for the comparatively low figure for consistency in classifying.[11]

In fact, library classification has long passed this primitive stage in its development, and, since the great work of Ranganathan in formulating his theory of facet analysis developed by B. C. Vickery and the Classification Research Group in London, it is now far from the primitive instrument it used to be. Ranganathan originally set out to devise a new scheme that would incorporate, consciously and systematically, the element of synthesis that had first appeared in DC as common subdivisions and geographical subdivisions. The Library of Congress, so dear to the heart of the practical chaps, rejected even this modest measure, but Brown in England and Bliss in the United States extended the device so that it enabled other complex subjects to be synthesized. But the fundamental contribution of Ranganathan is that he was the first to see that every term in a scheme must be a simple term, that classes should not be regarded as conglomerations of complex subjects but as sets of elements capable of combination with each other exactly as the literature itself required. His basic theoretical book, the *Prolegomena to Library Classification*,[12] is worked out in

---

[9] R. A. Fairthorne, *Towards Information Retrieval* (London: Butterworths, 1961).

[10] M. Taube and Associates, *Studies in Co-ordinate Indexing* (Washington, D.C.: Documentation, Inc., 1953), pp. 12, 35.

[11] H. Borko and Myrna Berwick, *Automatic Document Classification: Part II* (Santa Monica, Calif.: System Development Corporation, 1963).

[12] S. R. Ranganathan, *Prolegomena to Library Classification* (2d ed.; London: Library Association, 1957).

great detail, in mathematical fashion, strongly resembling Whitehead and Russell's *Principia Mathematica* in its presentation. It includes a critique of the other general schemes in the light of this theory.

This is a difficult work, however, and a less detailed and simpler exposition can be found in the *Philosophy of Library Classification*.[13] In these works, Ranganathan goes beyond the theory of facet analysis conceived simply as an arrangement of elementary terms into sets. He works out a general theory in which each set, or facet, contains terms all of which relate to a fundamental abstract category capable of realization in specific instances according to the context, or class. If we take geographical subdivision as a manifestation of the abstract category "Space," and chronological subdivision of the category "Time," Ranganathan contends that a system can be established to cover all phenomena with no more than five such categories. These he calls Personality, Matter, Energy, Space, and Time; and their application can be illustrated most simply by the classification of a technology. Personality represents the end product, the thing made, an entity having specific properties and purposes. Matter represents the raw material out of which it is made. Energy represents the operations applied to the raw material to make it.

This all-pervasive general theory has been, and is still being, further elaborated. It has much to offer as a starting point for subject analysis, although there has been little agreement with the fundamental categories outside of Ranganathan's own group in India. But the theory of facet analysis has been substantiated by a great deal of other work, mainly in Europe, but also in the United States and the U.S.S.R. Jessica Melton has made an interesting comparison between the Colon Classification and the WRU semantic code index, showing that, out of twenty-five basic ideas, nineteen are found to correspond in both systems, and the remainder show some degree of similarity.[14]

By allowing his fundamental categories to appear on more than one "level" in the same facet, and if necessary in more than one "round" of categories in the same basic class, Ranganathan surmounts the difficulty that many subjects have more than five facets. In Europe, where faceted classifications are in use in many special libraries and documentation centers, our approach has been more pragmatic. We have not attempted to identify our facets with fundamental categories but have retained the original idea of taking a class and grouping its terms into homogeneous, mutually exclusive sets, naming them as seems appropriate to the context. In England, the Classification Research Group, at the request of the Library Association, has just begun work on a new general scheme which will cover the whole of knowledge.[15]

Whatever their differences, all these schemes have a similar structure. Terms are sorted into facets, and then arranged as far as desirable in hierarchies, producing a traditional classi-

[13] S. R. Ranganathan, *Philosophy of Library Classification* (Copenhagen: E. Munksgaard, 1951).

[14] J. Melton, *A Note on the Compatibility of Two Information Systems, Colon Classification and Western Reserve University (Encoded Telegraphic Abstracts) and the Feasibility of Interchanging Their Notations* (Cleveland: Western Reserve, 1960).

[15] Library Association, *Some Problems of a General Classification Scheme: Report of a Conference Held in London, June 1963* (London: Library Association, 1964).

ficatory sequence; rules are made for combining the terms as required to name the subjects of documents; notational symbols are allocated to fix the terms automatically in a helpful sequence. Classifying documents is a process of analysis and synthesis: first the subject of the document is analyzed into its facets, and then the scheme is consulted, at each facet in turn, to find the terms and symbols that match the subject. The same process can be used for reference service, and it is clear that we now have a powerful instrument for insuring consistency, not only in classifying the documents that come into our collections but also in steering the thoughts of an inquirer into the same channels when formulating his request. Thus the librarian has a scheme that does not simply provide a code symbol for a subject after it has been identified but actively assists in the identification. I know from my own experience how useful readers find it when a librarian is able to put before them a systematic analysis of their subject, so that they can easily discover the right point of entry into the library's system.

In a faceted classification, relations between terms are settled by their relative positions, both within a facet and between facets. The sequence of facets identifies the nature of the terms in the same way as the sequence of words in a sentence. When I say "I saw Tom kiss Mary," the relationship between me and Mary is different from that between Tom and Mary, and this important difference is shown by the position of the various words in the sequence.

We have long felt the need for more precision in specifying relations in a classification scheme. Position in a sequence is but one way of doing this.

The teams at the United States Patent Office have developed their system of "interfixes"; Western Reserve has its "infixes" which express the relationship between a semantic factor and the specific topic coded and its separate "role indicators" which, as Vickery has shown, act as inflections in the same way as the case endings in an inflected language.[16]

An advanced theoretical study of the use of relationship symbols in an alphabetical system has been made by J. E. Farradane,[17] who also derives his system from work by experimental psychologists, including Piaget and J. P. Guilford of the University of Southern California. He considers that all such relationships can be grouped into nine categories, based on the functioning of the human brain in the formation of concepts. These can be related in two ways: as distinct or non-distinct one from another or in a time sequence. By adding a third co-ordinate—that of "Neither"—he produces his series of nine categories, which he then identifies with symbols, called "operators," that are found on a standard typewriter. Farradane is still developing this theory and has not yet produced a definitive account, but he has already produced several faceted classification schemes for special subjects, including, in collaboration with Vickery, that used at Cranfield and in the WRU-Cranfield tests. He does not derive his facet sequence by reference to Ranganathan's

[16] B. C. Vickery, *Classification and Indexing in Science* (2d ed.; London: Butterworths, 1959); and B. C. Vickery, *On Retrieval System Theory* (London: Butterworths, 1961).

[17] J. E. Farradane, "Fundamental Fallacies and New Needs in Classification," in *Essays in Librarianship in Memory of William Charles Berwick Sayers* (London: Library Association, 1961), pp. 120–35.

fundamental categories but by applying his operators, in their own sequence, to linking facets.

In the United States, much attention has been paid to the listing of terms in the form of a "thesaurus" of which there are currently at least four different meanings. Now the original thesaurus, of Roget, provided one of the sources of Ranganathan's idea of fundamental categories; Roget used more than five, but all his groups were based on abstract conceptions such as Relation, Quantity, Matter, and so on. Within each group, there is further subdivision, and many of these subdivisions are common to several groups: Abstract, Concrete, Relative. The whole is actually a scheme of classification, as indeed are those of its modern descendants that I have seen. The intention is the same as that of a faceted classification: to display a term in each of the contexts in which it may be found, together with the other terms found in those contexts. Most thesauruses have been produced to enable a machine to perform the transformation of author's terms or inquirer's terms into the terms used in the index consulted.

My present brief does not include consideration of the possibilities of mechanizing classification and indexing, but I should like to make a few brief comments on some new developments that have been introduced. I hope that we have now passed that first ecstatic decade, when it sometimes appeared as if the mere flaunting of a punched card, or better still a roll of magnetized tape, provided instant reference service without need of any system of subject analysis at all. The skepticism I have always felt about machine literature-searching—as distinct from data correlation—has received fresh encouragement from the WRU-Cranfield tests, but we are now, I think, asking the correct question: "What can the machines do for us?" instead of "What can we provide for the machine to do?"

There is clearly a promising field for application in one sphere of bibliography at least, the updating and printing out of lists of references. This technique is most appropriate for non-selective lists, such as the *British National Bibliography,* which uses punched cards to update a classified file of entries for scanning by a FotoList sequential camera and subsequent offset-lithographic printing.

Of the many other uses, perhaps the KWIC Indexes are most prominent just now. I find them repulsive to look at, but that is the fault of the printing head and not of the technique. The immediately attractive feature of a KWIC Index is that it provides multiple access; it is a faceted index of a sort because it provides an entry under each key word (of a title or a subject analysis), which usually turns out to represent the various facets of the subject. The permuting of the key words is done automatically, as it is in the permuted index to reports produced at the Whetstone Library of the English Electric Company, using the EEC KDP10 computer. Both of these are alphabetical indexes, though the English Electric refers to a classified file of reports; a KWIC Index could do the same, of course.

Automatic permutation could also be applied to a classified sequence, provided that it were based on a faceted classification. The technique would be the same, except that the arranging symbol would be a classification symbol and not the alphabet. This is illustrated in the series of examples published with *The London Education Classification;*[18] its advantage, in my view, is that each entry is arranged next to related topics and not, as in the KWIC Index, next to words that happen to be adjacent in the alphabet.

Much more could be said on the theoretical foundations of these methods. But it is time to sum up their role in education for librarianship. First, let us look at the subject from the point of view of the basic curriculum. Not every librarian needs to be able to make classification schemes, any more than he needs to be able to make a computer. But every librarian needs to understand the nature of the techniques he uses, and to judge the appropriateness of each to his own needs. For this, I suggest that the mere examination, in whatever detail, of the Decimal Classification or the Library of Congress Classification is hardly adequate. I suggest that classification and subject analysis, in the general sense of systematic concept co-ordination as I have discussed, consist of much more than the memorizing of arrangements that might have been found useful fifty years ago but which correspond only fortuitously to the complexities of documentation today. It is true that there are many schools of thought and great differences of opinion between them; by and large this is a healthy sign, so long as we remember that none of us is likely to be wholly correct and that those who disagree with us are not necessarily guilty of moral turpitude. For basic studies, the comparative analysis of current trends and theories offers much more toward establishing fundamental principles than the study of individual schemes in isolation, without reference to any theoretical background.

In advanced studies, I think there is no doubt that classification has established its claim to an important place. Although I have here described in detail only that work with which I have been connected myself, I have touched on much other work and still left vast areas without so much as a bare mention. Fortunately, one thing eminently distinguishes those who labor in this field of information retrieval: we have no objection to seeing ourselves in print. Even if, as has been unkindly said, the one subject on which few people bother to retrieve information is information retrieval, there is no lack of raw data. This widespread interest could not exist without the basis of a real need for systematic handling of information. Nor is this interest confined to librarians. At a recent meeting in London, a Classification Society was founded, mainly through the efforts of university scientists who have come to realize also that taxonomy, by itself, cannot cope with the manifold interpenetrations of natural phenomena. We hope that the society will provide a forum where experts in different branches of knowledge can discuss their own and each other's problems, in the hope of finding some common basic principles. Research, then, should aim at continuing such foundation studies, and library schools which exist in a university framework should find a home for such research. I am enough an Englishman to believe that even those lines of thought that appear to be most innocent of all practical taint may very well, in the end, uncover the key that will unlock the door to a whole new

---

[18] D. J. Foskett, *The London Education Classification* (London: Institute of Education, London University, 1963).

era. Let us, therefore, cultivate our gardens, even if we are not yet in the best of all possible worlds, for who knows upon whose head the apple may fall? And how many apples fell before the event chanced to be observed by a prepared mind?

Eighty-eight years ago, on September 12, 1876, that great Englishman Thomas Henry Huxley delivered the address at the opening of the Johns Hopkins University. He spoke of university education and of the necessity of linking basic research with the practical needs of the community and looked forward to the day when scholars would come to the American universities "from all parts of the earth, as of old they sought Bologna, or Paris, or Oxford." That day has come, and I think I cannot do better than to conclude by quoting Huxley's concluding words, both for their prophetic ring and for their appropriateness today.

"And it is pleasant to me to fancy," he said, "that, among the English students who are drawn to you at that time, there may linger a dim tradition that a countryman of theirs was permitted to address you as he has done today, and to feel as if your hopes were his hopes and your success his joy."

COMMENT

HAROLD BORKO

The paper to which Mr. Foskett referred is one of a series of experiments which some of my colleagues and I have been conducting at the System Development Corporation while studying the problems inherent in automated document classification. In this particular experiment, we compared two mathematical techniques for classifying documents into categories. One method involved the use of Bayesian prediction formulas; the other was based upon factor analysis and the use of factor scores for assigning classification categories. In order to make the comparative test of these two techniques as rigorous as possible, we set as our criterion the prediction of the most correct category; that is to say, each document had to be classified into one category only. Obviously, it was recognized that some documents could fit reasonably well into more than one category. However, the study was designed to test the efficiency of as yet unproven techniques for automated document classification. In conducting such tests, it behooves the experimenter to make his standards as stringent as possible. After the experimental techniques have been adequately tested and their effectiveness has been demonstrated, the restraints imposed by laboratory conditions can be relaxed.

Foskett was correct in pointing out that, in our insistence that each document be classified into the one most relevant category, we were being somewhat unrealistic and "primitive." Also, as he stated, this criterion contributed to the comparatively low, though still statistically significant, percentages of correct classification that were obtained. The differences in viewpoint arise from the fact that we were dealing with a laboratory experiment, while Foskett was describing operational procedures.

THE LIBRARIAN'S ROLE IN THE DEVELOPMENT OF LIBRARY BOOK COLLECTIONS

GORDON WILLIAMS

THE library's book collection—which we define here as all the written records in the library regardless of form—is of great importance in the total library economy. But however important it may be, it is only a part of this total. Therefore it is impossible to discuss it critically (and hence the librarian's role in its development) without a clear understanding of its relationship to the other parts that make up the total. The relationship of these parts is, in turn, determined by the purpose that the library is expected to accomplish. Let us, then, examine the purpose of the library as closely as possible, or rather let us try to determine what the purpose of the library is in terms that will help us most effectively to achieve that purpose.

TRADITIONAL GOALS

It might seem that this has been done so often that it need not be done again; yet I am certain that, if you ask the first half-dozen librarians you meet what the purpose of the library is, you will not get an immediate response, and that the responses you do get—after a lapse of several minutes in each case—will differ fundamentally. To some extent, these answers will represent legitimate differences of opinion, but the answers will also reflect an uncertainty that we need to recognize and make explicit. The primary uncertainty that I have in mind is the proper expression of the library's purpose in terms of information or of written records.

Throughout their history, libraries have been so concerned with written records that a definition based upon objective observation of their performance would probably be "to collect written records, to preserve them, and to make them available." Yet this definition is insufficient because it gives no hint as to why this should be desirable. In fact, written records are usually desirable because of the meanings the words can communicate to anyone who can read them; what is wanted is what we may call, for lack of a better term, the intellectual content of the words. Fundamentally, the written record itself is merely a carrier, a vehicle; and it is what is carried, not the carrier, that is usually of primary importance. But although libraries have collected books for their intellectual content, it is not accurate to say that the library has expressed its purpose as that of collecting, preserving, and disseminating information. At least, libraries have not so far done this. What libraries in fact do is to collect and organize the written records themselves, and when a searcher comes seeking information they say, in effect: "Here are the written records we have. That group over there may contain the information you want, but you must look for it yourself; and we cannot say that anything you may find is either accurate or inaccurate, nor can we assure you that that group contains all of the information pertinent to your inquiry, or even all that the library may have that is pertinent."

The point is that the library has not in the past been, and with very minor exceptions is not now, an "information center"; instead it was, and is, a record center. Its operation has been only to collect records and to help people find records. Until relatively recently this operation was the only one required. The scholar was presumed to know the literature of his subject, and indeed it was this knowledge that constituted scholarship. The scholar was primarily a literary man; his knowledge was a knowledge of books and of what they contained. He asked of a library not that it provide him with information, but that it provide him with a copy of the book he asked for; from this he would get the information he wanted. This system worked very well as long as scholarship was concerned primarily with classical subjects and as long as the number of works was small and grew slowly. But as man's knowledge and interests expanded, as observation and experiment replaced speculation, as general and quantifiable theorems replaced the rules of thumb, the form and content of education also expanded. Classical education remained, of course, but to this were added the natural and social sciences and technology; and written records of observations, explanation, and practice increased at least proportionately with education and interests. It was inevitable that library book collections should reflect this change, for libraries were the keepers of the records; but librarians did not fully perceive the change in patterns of use that accompanied this change in the records.

I do not mean, of course, that libraries or librarians have been unaware of the fundamental purpose of written records or unconcerned with the contents of the books they collect, but simply that their operations for the most part have been limited to the collection, preservation, and manipulation of books rather than of ideas. In large part, this limitation originated in the predominantly unitary nature of most books: that is, in most cases they were intended by their authors to be read in their entirety. This applied not only to works of the imagination—such as poetry, tales, drama, philosophy—but also to works intended to be primarily narrative or descriptive, as in history, biography, and even early science and technology. This emphasis on the whole book was reinforced by the relatively small number of books available. Neither the number or nature of the books themselves nor the ways in which they were commonly used called for significant assistance to the reader. But to help readers locate books, libraries very early in their history began to arrange them so that those dealing with the same general subject were shelved together. The size of library collections increased with the increase in the number of books, and this increase in turn forced a refinement in classification schemes. But the orientation of the system remained toward whole books as the unit of classification; it was the books themselves that were arranged in accordance with the classification.

THE RISE OF THE JOURNAL TO IMPORTANCE

Underlying the development of more detailed classification schemes was, of course, the need to accommodate larger collections. But the primary factor in the development was the growing, if somewhat vague, realization that a change was taking place in scholarly interests and in the reader's knowledge and the conclusion from this awareness that the reader would benefit by a scheme of classification that would aid him to locate not books but information.

But however refined the scheme, the classification of books was ill suited to the purpose because a book can be put in only one place regardless of the diverse information it contains. The solution to this dilemma was the subject, or classed, catalog, which made it possible to enter a work under more than one subject. Unfortunately, this solution came too late. A major shift from the publication of the monographic book to the publication of the journal had begun earlier and was growing rapidly—more rapidly than librarians or scholars had realized. Unlike the monograph, the journal contained the writings of many authors on discrete subjects only generally related to each other. Ideally these articles should have been published as pamphlets, and indeed many scholars treated them as such in their personal libraries by collecting the articles in the form of offprints from the journals. The journal itself was far too obvious a misfit to be comfortably accommodated within the libraries' classification schemes. But the rapid growth of journal publication had been unheeded so that by the time libraries were even partially aware of the problem, adequate solutions to it were beyond the resources of the library staffs.

I know of no statistics on the relative proportion of serial volumes to monographic volumes in libraries a hundred, or even fifty, years ago, but it must have been relatively small. Fussler and Simon's study of the patterns of use in large research libraries indicates that, as of now, perhaps half their volumes are serials. We can also guess that each serial volume probably contains a minimum of about twenty-five articles. In other words, for libraries to have cataloged individual articles as they did monographs would have resulted in at least a thirteen-fold increase in cataloging work load and a resulting increase in library staff. I doubt that this staff increase would have occurred had librarians ever begun such extensive cataloging, for I think other solutions would have been found. But by the time everyone became aware of the problem, it had become so large that libraries merely continued the methods they had been using. But because they did not solve the problem, research libraries now provide neither classification nor subject analysis for about half the volumes in their present collections. Meanwhile, the increasing number of written records resulted in the readers' need for more exact guides to the location of the information they wanted. This situation was not a change in the fundamental nature of the readers' needs. Readers have always wanted written records for what those records communicated—whether it was the poetry of Donne, the philosophy of Chuang Tsu, the history of the trade from Amsterdam in the year 1246, the life-history of the bristle-thighed Curlew, or instructions on how to calculate the orbit of Venus. But the readers now needed a more exact guide to the location of such information. Classification schemes brought together books on the same general subject, or of the same general type and language in the case of literary works, but they ignored the no-less-important articles in journals and serials. In any case, the accumulation of an increasing number of publications made it more and more difficult for the user to find the specific information he wanted.

Neither the library nor the librarian could give the information requested efficiently, particularly if the information was not available in monographs owned by the library. But since it was essential that the information be found, scholars themselves began to produce indexes and abstracts of the periodical literature. It is pertinent to note one major distinction between library classification and subject cataloging on the one hand, and the published periodical index on the other. This is that, with few and generally minor exceptions, the periodical indexes are not based on the collection in any one library. Instead they usually attempt to include as many of the existing periodicals that publish material pertinent to the purpose of the index as they can find. The success of this attempt varies from index to index, but the distinction between coverage based on some particular collection and coverage based on the existing literature is valid. This distinction emphasizes the magnitude of the shift in the needs of both the scholarly and the general reader from need of access to written records to need of guidance in the location of particular kinds of information. At the same time, the traditional role of the library in keeping records and helping readers find particular records, rather than giving them particular information, is confirmed. Libraries do classify the monographs in their collections, do give them some deliberately limited subject cataloging, and do help readers in varying degrees to find what they want. Yet libraries generally have not attempted in the past, and do not attempt now, to make their own guides to published records either as broad in coverage irrespective of location or as detailed in analysis of individual works as those guides the scholar has provided for himself through his various societies and associations, and in some cases even through his own individual efforts.

The steady accumulation of knowledge and of written records has had two other quite opposite effects, particularly on university libraries and only to a degree lesser on other libraries. The individual has reacted to the growth of information in the only way so far possible—by increasing specialization on a smaller portion of the whole. But this reaction was not possible for the university or for society generally, and consequently not for the libraries created to serve their needs. The university has not narrowed its curriculum. On the contrary it has continually broadened its interests and activities to include the study of more and more specialties. The effect of this broadening has been to increase the total demand on both university libraries serving students and faculty and on the public and special libraries serving the universities' graduates. These factors, separately and in combination, have resulted in tensions that seem destined either to reshape the library significantly or to create a new instrument of uncertain relationship to the traditional library. The sharper segregation of interest into narrower, and therefore more numerous, specialties has created more interfaces. This, plus the growing number of records, has made necessary more than guides to the location of records. It has made necessary guides to the information in the records that neither the library nor any other agency is yet satisfactorily providing. At the same time, the total range of interest has broadened, requiring access to more records than any one library, under present conditions, can conceivably supply from its own collections.

One can imagine a time in the future when technology and copyright laws will make it possible for every library to have in its own collection a copy of every published written record. However, there are as yet no economically feasible techniques in sight for accomplishing this, although the Council on Library Resources has sent several scouts ahead specifically to look for them. Until such a collection is possible, a library can have only a selection of the existing written records, and (although this is less certain) the selection will probably be an increasingly smaller proportion of the total that is extant.

In this brief and oversimplified review I wish to emphasize that we must recognize and accept the fact that the information needs of everyone—humanist, scientist, and ordinary citizen —are now substantially different from what they were a hundred or more years ago, but that the techniques and organization used by the library to satisfy these needs are not substantially different from what they were then. More important, they are fundamentally inadequate to satisfy the present needs. If we are willing to accept the proposition that the demands for published information and for records that will enrich people intellectually and emotionally are to be satisfied by the library, then we must accept the proposition that every library is responsible for locating and making available to its patrons any published information they require, a proposition that has not been hitherto acknowledged.

The restriction of the responsibility to "published" information is a necessary limitation: unless the information has been published it is either impossible or illegal for libraries to provide it. The concept requires further that not only must a matter be made public but that it also must be recorded, although any form of recording will suffice. The proposition is not intended to include whatever exists, at any given moment, only in the mind of one or more persons.

It might seem that this statement also requires the qualification, "it is the library's legitimate purpose to provide," but a second thought will show that no information can be foreseen to be foreign to the library's purpose. Libraries, of course, do recognize some limitations on what it is their legitimate purpose to provide, but they put this limitation not on the possible range of information but on the patron they serve and on his purpose. The university library, for example, does not believe that it has a responsibility to provide information on the batting averages of the Chicago White Sox in 1910 in order to satisfy the sports interest of a professor of classics. But the same library does have a responsibility to provide this information for the graduate student in the Department of Education writing a doctoral dissertation on "The Relation between the Batting Averages of Professional Baseball Players and Their High-School Grades in English Composition." In every case where a library might say that it is not its legitimate purpose to provide such and such information, I believe that analysis will show that judgment to be based not on the information itself but on the inquirer or on his purpose. It must be noted also that the library's responsibility to make any published information available logically implies the responsibility to make all published information available. Unless it has the ability to make all published information available, it can supply the reader's need only for some information.

But partly because of their historical orientation and partly because only relatively recently have technological advances made it possible, libraries have never specifically accepted this responsibility of making available *any* information their patrons require. Instead they have unconsciously substituted as their major responsibility what was originally merely the best means of satisfying this need, but is no longer, namely the addition to their own collection of as many records as possible. And we must emphasize that libraries have recognized no theoretical limit to such additions, so that the substitution of the phrase *any information* for the phrase *any record* is not a change in the library's presently accepted limits. It indicates, rather, a fundamental change in viewpoint that, if adopted, significantly changes the quantity that the several classes of library expenditure are balanced to maximize. It is the nature of this rebalancing that we must now consider.

IDENTIFY, LOCATE, AND DELIVER

In order for a library to put before a patron any published information he wants, it must perform three distinct operations. It must identify the record containing this information; it must locate a copy of the record; and it must get the desired information to the patron.

Now for the library to identify the record, or records, containing any published information a patron may need, a library must have a comprehensive index to all published information and not merely to that information in the library receiving the request. What is required is a bibliographic guide that enables one to identify every published record, regardless of its form, by useful characteristics, or a combination of characteristics, related to the information it carries. These characteristics include not only those commonly used now, such as author, title, imprint, and the general subject with which it deals, but a much finer and wider range of characteristics that requires a more detailed analysis of content than is now common. Both to produce and to make available to every library such a comprehensive guide may seem, to some, so practically impossible as to be fit only for discussion in the least responsible of the Sunday newspaper supplements or description in utopian fiction. Complete achievement certainly is not likely within the foreseeable future, but I think it is certain that, using only presently available methods, this is possible for a much larger portion of information than is now provided. Furthermore, the cost of such a comprehensive guide is not beyond the reach of presently available funds, provided only that librarians and scholars will make the effort and adjustments necessary to accomplish it. This conclusion is not based on what computers can and probably will do for libraries in the near future, but only on what librarians' heads and hands could do now with the typewriter, camera, and printing press, if these heads and hands were directed toward doing only once what they now do repetitively. That computers will almost certainly increase the speed and ease of doing and distributing this work is important and exciting, but a significant increase in the availability of information is not dependent upon them alone. To appreciate this one need only ask how many libraries would have a tool even approaching the depth of analysis and breadth of coverage of *Chemical Abstracts* if each library had to produce it for itself. Indeed, two conclusions about the use of computers seem almost certain. First, the possible increase in the availability of information through the use of computers alone is less than the increase in the availability of information through proper co-ordination of the human effort on which the computers ultimately depend. Second, even what increase computers can contribute will be small unless there is effective co-ordination of this effort.

The second general operation required after identifying the record wanted is that of locating a copy of it. In present library practice this information is sometimes gained at the same time the record is identified, but not invariably so. Even if the identification is made in the library's card catalog, the record may be in use, it may be lost or at the bindery, or, if a serial, the library may own only a part of it but not the part wanted at this moment. If the record has been identified in some other source, the location of copies may be given, as in the National Union Catalog, or implied, as in the British Museum Catalog; but frequently, as in many periodical indexes and abstracts, no location is given, and this information must be determined in a completely separate operation. Two points need to be noted specifically with respect to information about the location of records. The first is that any source that can identify a record can simultaneously give the location of at least one copy of it. The second point is that the only purpose in making the location of a record generally known is to make it available to any person who needs it. Together these factors indicate that location both can and ought to be intimately related to identification and that the number of locations necessary is a function of the freedom and speed with which the records are available to users.

The third general operation, to which the first two are merely necessary preludes, is putting the information before the person wanting it. While it is not invariably necessary that the published record carrying this information, or even a copy of it, be put before him, for some purposes only the original record or an acceptable copy of it can give the information desired, so the ability to supply it is therefore required.

MAKING RECORDS AVAILABLE

As already stated, there is no presently practical expectation of any library's having in its own store an example in original form, or even some kind of copy, of every written record. Until this is not only a practical possibility but an accomplished fact, libraries can satisfy the requirement for the availability of every record only by having some system that assures every library of reasonably prompt access to every record, or an acceptable copy of it, that it cannot provide from its own collection. In specific terms, every library must be able to acquire promptly and readily—by loan or purchase—from elsewhere every record, or an acceptable copy of it, that it cannot readily put before the patron from its own store.

The desirability of this is not a new concept. Libraries have reluctantly used interlibrary loan programs for several years now (but not for as long as some of us may think: the first ALA

Interlibrary Loan Code was promulgated only in 1917 and was not revised again until 1940). They have even initiated a co-ordinated acquisition program, the Farmington Plan, to try to insure a readily borrowable copy within the United States of every publication of importance from a selected group of foreign countries. But far more important, libraries generally have not yet made any serious attempt to make records that are located in other libraries as nearly as possible as available as those they have locally. In more general terms, they have not yet fully accepted that their fundamental responsibility is to locate and make available to their patrons all published information and not merely those records that they can individually afford to buy and individually coarsely classify as whole units. The consequence of this is that they have not yet so allocated their budgets and energies to fulfil this responsibility to the maximum degree.

The only reason for a library to add records to its own collection is so that the records its present and future patrons want will be available to them as quickly as possible. The addition of records to a library costs money, and we can therefore say that a library spends money in order to make as many records as possible quickly available to its patrons. We ought, therefore, to judge the efficiency of any particular expenditure by how well it accomplishes this purpose. In practice, libraries add many records to their collections in advance of any explicitly known need and only in anticipation of a need that may arise quickly, that may arise many years from now, or may not arise at all in that particular library. The proportion of records added to a library merely in anticipation of a possible need is, in some cases, very substantial. We still do not know nearly as much about patterns of use of records as we would like to, but we do have pertinent data on the use of serials in two large and heavily used collections.

The John Crerar Library recently kept a record of all serial titles requested during a twelve-month period and discovered that 65 per cent of the approximately 11,000 serial titles it receives currently were not used even once during that period.[1] Note that the unit being counted in this instance was the title itself and not merely the current year's issues, and that this study showed no use of any issue, old or new, of 65 per cent of the titles the library subscribes to currently. Roughly similar figures were reported by the National Library of Medicine in its study of its interlibrary loan service.[2] These NLM figures are not quite comparable to the Crerar's because they are based on interlibrary loan use only, not local use; but there is considerable evidence that, in this case, local patrons and interlibrary loan patrons use essentially the same titles. Because of this we can use the NLM data as at least tending to confirm Crerar's. Over a longer period of time, more than 35 per cent of the titles will be used, of course, but it costs the library a substantial amount of money each year it keeps the title, adding still more to the cost of having material at hand only for immediate use in case of need.

Let us now look beyond this to see

[1] Margaret Notheisen, "A Study of the Use of Serials at the John Crerar Library" (unpublished Master's thesis, Graduate Library School, University of Chicago, 1960).

[2] William H. Kurth, *Survey of the Interlibrary Loan Operation of the National Library of Medicine* (Washington, D.C.: U.S. Public Health Service, 1962).

what happens when a patron wants a specific serial title not owned by his library. It is not uncommon for a scholarly library to spend $70,000 a year on wrong guesses of serial titles its patrons will want, and it does this only to provide quick availability. The question is: What will it do when the patron wants a title it lacks? If the patron is an undergraduate student the library will, usually, do nothing at all for him, though it makes no distinction between the undergraduates, graduates, and faculty in allowing use of the serial titles it does have. If the patron is a graduate student, *and* if he is working on a dissertation, or if he is a member of the faculty, the library will try to borrow the title for him on interlibrary loan, but it will pay nothing to get this for him as quickly as possible, though speed of access is the primary reason for spending money to acquire materials for its own collection. And not only will it not now spend money on a long-distance phone call, or first-class airmail delivery, to get the record for him tomorrow or the day after instead of two or three weeks from now, but if it cannot borrow the record at all, which is likely in the case of serials, it usually will not pay for a photocopy but will make the patron do so himself. In terms of the purpose for which the library's money is being spent, to provide as quick availability as possible for as many records as possible, would not a better system be to reduce somewhat the number of titles being subscribed to for possible use sometime, and then to spend the money thus saved on getting within twenty-four or forty-eight hours what the patron actually wants now? I think there can be little doubt that this would provide better service to patrons for the money expended.

It is also important that libraries recognize that their borrowing from another source to meet a patron's present need should not be limited to "infrequently used materials," since usage is now commonly measured only from the libraries' points of view. That is, this term now ordinarily applies to the frequency with which a library's patrons, taken as a whole, use a particular book. But from a patron's point of view, the frequency of use of any particular book is how many times *he* uses it within any given period of time. Some books—for example, dictionaries, encyclopedias, and bibliographies—are frequently used from both points of view, but only slightly beyond this small core of books the points of view yield different results, and the further we go beyond this core the more they differ. The reason for this is that beyond the quite small group of books that a particular patron uses more than once, far and away the majority of works that he uses, he uses only once.

Consider, for example, the case of two different books in a particular library, one of which is used by an average of four different people each year for several years and another which is used in that library only once every fifty years. To the library, the first book is very frequently used and the second is very infrequently used, but to the patron who uses them, both are used with equal frequence—that is, once. If we accept the proposition that the library exists to serve the needs of its patrons, then ideally both books ought to be equally readily available to the patron when he wants them. But since no library can conceivably have in its own collection all of the written records its patrons might possibly want at any given moment, it is manifestly impossible for all records to be equally readily available to them.

In terms of library efficiency it is obviously better for the library to have in its own collection the records that it will be asked for most frequently from its point of view, and to get as quickly as possible from elsewhere those that it may have to borrow only once every twenty-five or fifty years, or even less frequently. On the average, this choice will also be better even for every individual library patron, since the books most frequently used from the library's point of view are also the majority of the books any individual patron uses. To put this another way, most of the books any particular patron uses are also used by many other patrons; only a minority of the books that any particular patron uses are used only by him. This fact accounts for the variability in frequency of use as measured from the library's point of view. If this were not true, then all of the library's books would be used with approximately the same frequency. But from the point of view of the individual patron it makes no difference why a particular book is not immediately available from the library's collection. Whether the book is not in the collection because it is asked for only once every fifty years, or because it is lost, at the bindery, or another patron has it, it is equally unavailable for immediate use when he wants it. This means that, in the interest of the service to patrons that libraries are spending their money to provide, they should not only be more willing to duplicate frequently used books but that they should also be more able and more willing to borrow quickly whatever they cannot for any reason supply from their own collections.

NEED TO REBALANCE EXPENDITURES

I am not trying to suggest that a library need have nothing in its collection that is not used at least once a year. I am suggesting only that the immediate reason a library adds books to its collection is to make as many books as possible as readily available as possible when wanted, and that money spent both to make more records available on interlibrary loan, and to make interlibrary loan much faster, will give better library service even if some of this money must come from the present book budget. But to make this shift practical there must first be an assured system for every library to get what it cannot immediately provide from some other place that is stocked, staffed, and organized to give the fast kind of service just described. For some materials this may be other libraries that are, like themselves, placing primary emphasis on service to local individuals, but a number of considerations indicate that for a very great number of materials one or more centers especially established to give this service will be much more efficient than a division of responsibility among individual libraries. We need not try to prove this now, for the exact form of the system is less important than that the system work effectively; and there is no question that this is possible in one form or another.

Neither need we at this moment inquire whether this system should be paid for wholly or in part by the federal government, or whether it should be paid for from library budgets. For the most part there is only one primary source for the money required. Whether society provides it directly for this purpose, or indirectly through the libraries themselves, is at least theoretically indifferent. In practice, however, it is far from indifferent, for federal support can more equally distribute both the costs and the benefits. Yet regardless of the direct source of funds libraries must establish and supervise the pattern; and, more important to our immediate consideration, the librarian must determine the balance between (1) guides to the location of information and of records containing it, (2) records in the local collection, and (3) records in another but accessible location, that makes the maximum amount of information in published records most readily available to the library's patrons.

This is the librarian's role with respect to the development of book collections. Since, given any budget limitation—and there always is one—a decision to spend a dollar to add a book to the local collection is also a decision not to spend a dollar for a better guide to the location of information within books, and not to spend a dollar for better availability of what is not immediately available in the local collection. The librarian cannot reasonably develop a local book collection without considering these alternatives.

It is true that today it is easier for the librarian to spend his money on a book than on the alternatives, but this is an essential part of his problem. He must first design a library system embracing all libraries—practically, all libraries in the United States as his first approximation—that will achieve the best balance, both over all and within individual library budgets, and then establish the system. Only then can he begin to rebalance his own local library expenditures for maximum benefit to his patron's needs.

We can illustrate part of this rebalancing by referring again to *Chemical Abstracts*. Probably few librarians have stopped for long enough their swearing at the *Chemical Abstracts* system for identifying serial titles, and their thinking of how many more journals they could add to their own collection if *Chemical Abstracts* cost them only seventy dollars a year instead of seven hundred, to make a supposition and then ask themselves a question. Suppose that the library's total budget—its budget for acquisitions, personnel, equipment, etc.—is fixed at exactly what it is now in every library and that *Chemical Abstracts* does not exist. Given these conditions, we could conclude that the library now receiving *Chemical Abstracts* might have in its library as many more journals as seven hundred dollars would pay for, including in this cost that of the subscription itself plus the cost of ordering, paying invoices, cataloging, checking in, claiming, binding, etc. Let us make a minimal estimate and say that the annual cost per title, including all of these factors, is ten dollars per title, even though the average is probably much more. The library would have in its collection, then, seventy more serial titles than it now does. Now let us suppose that *Chemical Abstracts* is suddenly offered for subscription for seven hundred dollars a year and the only way the library can acquire it is to cut seventy journals from its subscription list. Which choice gives the library's patrons the greater amount of information that the library fundamentally exists to provide? Is the better choice "x-thousand and seventy" journals, a great many of them in foreign languages not easily read and browsed through by the library's patrons, even if they had the time; distributed widely through the library, some with chemistry, some with physiology, some with medicine, some with engineering, etc.; and with no guide, subject or otherwise, to the articles in these journals, but with only two entries in the card catalog for the journal itself, one under its title, and one under some such heading as "Chemistry. Periodicals," or "Physiology. Periodicals"? Or is it a better choice to have only the "x-thousand" journals plus abstracts, usually in English, of about 100,000 articles of chemical interest from these journals, plus several thousand others, each entered under an average of twenty-four specific subject headings, together with a reference to the journal containing it, and a rough guide to where copies are located in the United States? I think the better choice is obvious, but if librarians have any doubts let them ask their patrons.

If the choice for *Chemical Abstracts* is as obvious and unanimous as I think, then let me ask another question. Suppose it is not *Chemical Abstracts* that is suddenly offered for sale but the availability of a bibliographic tool of comparable, or even improved, scope for English literature, American history, European history, economics, anthropology, meteorology, or for any subject you care to name, and covering monographs as well as serials. Is your answer still the same? Remember that with this improved access to the intellectual contents of written records, and as an integral part of the whole system, we are also proposing a much easier and faster access to the records that are not themselves in the individual library's own collection. Remember, too, that with the addition of more detailed and centrally prepared guides to the intellectual content of monographs and to their identification, the substantial savings in local cataloging costs will also help pay for the increased service.

The point I wish to emphasize is that the alternatives last offered are not imaginary. In similar terms they exist today with this difference only: instead of these services being offered to libraries if they will pay their money, libraries must take the initiative and offer their money and the system first. Several libraries must make the offer simultaneously, and the librarians must, with this money, establish the organization to do the work. The problems in doing this are complex and difficult but not insoluble. The most essential requirement is a change in the librarian's view of the functions that society's needs—and the number and nature of written records—now require libraries to perform and of the most effective way for libraries to fulfil these functions. It is, in other words, a change in the quantity that library expenditures are balanced to maximize. And let me also emphasize that although I have spoken, by way of illustration, of reducing the number of books or journals a library might acquire in order to provide something else that will make the library more useful to its patrons, I do not mean that I think libraries are now acquiring too many materials. I think even more would be desirable. I am referring only to the relative *balance* between expenditures in each of the categories of library operation as this now commonly obtains within any given total library budget, and as this balance might be within that, or any other total budget, in order to provide the maximum satisfaction of patron needs. The absolute amount spent in each category may well rise, and in fact probably will have to in order to meet society's requirements. The librarian's role, however, is not to build the largest book collection but to determine and obtain the best balance, with whatever amount is available, that makes the maximum amount of information available most readily to his library's patrons.